Transforming Education

Transforming Education

Building Foundations for Systemic Change and Empowered Communities

Quintin Shepherd

ROWMAN & LITTLEFIELD
Lanham • Boulder • New York • London

Published by Rowman & Littlefield
An imprint of The Rowman & Littlefield Publishing Group, Inc.
4501 Forbes Boulevard, Suite 200, Lanham, Maryland 20706
www.rowman.com

86-90 Paul Street, London EC2A 4NE

Copyright © 2024 by Quintin Shepherd

All rights reserved. No part of this book may be reproduced in any form or by any electronic or mechanical means, including information storage and retrieval systems, without written permission from the publisher, except by a reviewer who may quote passages in a review.

British Library Cataloguing in Publication Information Available

Library of Congress Cataloging-in-Publication Data

Names: Shepherd, Quintin, author.
Title: Transforming education : building foundations for systemic change and empowered communities / Quintin Shepherd.
Description: Lanham, Maryland : Rowman & Littlefield Publishers, 2024. | Includes bibliographical references.
Identifiers: LCCN 2023044574 (print) | LCCN 2023044575 (ebook) | ISBN 9781475874082 (cloth) | ISBN 9781475874099 (paperback) | ISBN 9781475874105 (ebook)
Subjects: LCSH: School districts—United States—Administration. | School superintendents—United States. | School boards—United States. | Educational leadership—United States. | Educational change—United States.
Classification: LCC LB2817.3 .S53 2024 (print) | LCC LB2817.3 (ebook) | DDC 379.1/5350973—dc23/eng/20231024
LC record available at https://lccn.loc.gov/2023044574
LC ebook record available at https://lccn.loc.gov/2023044575

Contents

Foreword	vii
Introduction: Transformation: An Aspiration, Moral Imperative, or a Goal?	1
Chapter 1: Equitable Funding Structures	15
Chapter 2: Quality Assurance and a Cadence of Accountability	31
Chapter 3: Fostering Community-Wide Ownership of Learning	47
Chapter 4: Courageous Leadership and Policymaking	63
Chapter 5: Cultivate Public Will and Understanding for Transformation	83
Chapter 6: Participatory Budgeting	99
Chapter 7: Case Study: Victoria Independent School District	115
Chapter 8: Final Thoughts for Superintendents	131
Chapter 9: Final Thoughts for Board Members	145
Bibliography	157
Acknowledgments	167
About the Author	169

Foreword

I have had the honor of serving the education sector for the better part of almost three decades. My work has been in administration at the elementary level. I've worked as adjunct faculty in higher education, as a curriculum designer, guest lecturer, and, most notably, as a media member privileged to cover the people, places, and changemakers dotting the global education landscape. This extended background either means I've earned my gray hair or narrowly survived the trials and tribulations of an industry in constant flux.

Because of the gales challenging the very tenets of education, I can lean into the personalities guiding change throughout the sector. The media, while vitriolized, can serve the purpose of clarification during times of uncertainty. Most communities look to district leadership to chart a course that serves multiple functions: create a culture that attracts and keeps talented educators, develop community relationships centered on inclusiveness and active engagement, and generate solutions to tackle the realities of public education while harnessing the opportunities carefully fostered by leaders steeped in humility and intention.

I met Quintin Shepherd through an interview that led to another interview and several calls falling into the category of, "just because." I recognized a similar feed-the-beast mentality in Quintin that I personally thrive on. His penchant for new data points, conversations, and opportunities to expand his professional horizon was and continues to be second to none from my seat as a proud chronicler of stories in education.

You might wonder if my assessment of the author could be applied industry-wide. Like Quintin, I owe it to you, the reader and assumed steward of education's role in society, to be honest: Most of my conversations with district leaders feel less empowering and more like a sales pitch because the job of superintendent has become increasingly political and flashy.

I go back to my acknowledgment of Quintin's first book (*The Secret to Transformational Leadership*) that publishers kindly graced the cover with, "Dr. Quintin Shepherd's humility draws us in, sharpens our focus, and opens our eyes to how our words impact those around us. Every change requires an accelerant—and Quintin kindles the flame inside every leader who wants to be the difference."

Why invoke past praise? Education is about stacking together experiences of knowledge transformation into wheels of progress, guiding us to points along our life's journey, bringing clarity and wonderment. Those who embrace personal empowerment unlock professional impact statements documenting the steps needed to share opportunities across cultures of difference, creating communities of meaning. Quintin's latest book ignites colorfully rich imaginations through his artful prose, positioning the reader in the middle of the Amazon, on a dance floor, and at the drafting table as the architect of educational and inclusive change.

Quintin's layered journey takes us around the world and into the crevices of our humanity, exposing the richness of humility to better serve poignant professional relationships and experiences to enrich local communities. One of, if not the essential, collaboration tools of leaders district-wide remains the active or stale relationship status a superintendent has with their school board.

When Quintin approached me about writing the foreword to this book, I leaped at the chance. I have been privy to so many conversations with superintendents and school board members but rarely together and rarely without conflict. A not-so-subtle secret in education is the pivotal nature of district success related to the collaborative achievements between superintendents and school boards. As a result, there are few submissions in the annals of education that draft a blueprint of inclusion among these leadership layers.

As you turn each page of Quintin's book, a blueprint will emerge, providing definitions to shared experiences and new methods to better understand your individual role in the tried-and-true exchanges between leaders that can derail progress. You'll be challenged to think twice about myopic viewpoints and gain clarity on the core difference between listening and hearing and the very frame of reference needed to secure a perspective on critical relationship criteria for success.

In the classic holiday movie, *It's a Wonderful Life*, George Bailey, played by Jimmy Stewart, gains perspective from the balcony of life. Quintin, like Bailey, gives the reader a sense that he's sitting next to you, overlooking your district or community leadership in action, noting the observable patterns needing an oil change of context. Quintin is both your friend and mentor on the journey to creating sustainable relationships and systems foundational to successful educational outcomes.

Given that you are reading this opening salvo of this book by Quintin, I am going to go out on a limb and wager that you, like so many, are actively scanning the horizon for guidance to serve your local communities better. In my humble opinion, leadership and opportunities to lead can be found or sought after. Understanding our current personal and professional boundaries, either in talent or perspective, sheds light on the elemental and humble ingredients necessary for leadership to thrive.

I have had a front-row seat to many US education leaders, interviewing hundreds of district administrators, award-winning educators, university chancellors, ministers of education from several countries, and the former US secretary of education Arne Duncan. I consciously leave hyperbole on the sideline when I say that Quintin Shepherd represents the best of us, casting a shadow large enough for others to share in. He is an inclusive and incredibly reflective leader who doesn't have to share his thoughts in a book or on a stage but does because of the generations on the rise. Quintin doesn't care if he rattles a few institutional cages on his way to substantive change—and not for the sheer purpose of change but for a growing knowledge base of people and cultures he rightly celebrates in service.

I encourage readers to tackle conventional wisdom and ask a simple question while treating Quintin's book like your permanent and professional carry-on baggage: Are the choices I'm contemplating empowering for those I am in service of, or are they limiting in scope and creativity?

Humbly,
Rod Berger, PsyD

Introduction

Transformation: An Aspiration, Moral Imperative, or a Goal?

Is school and district transformation an aspiration, a moral imperative, or a goal? Moreover, what exactly is transformational leadership, and how do you know when you are doing it? Finally, how can we build supportive systemic structures in school districts to support transformational change and leadership? These are the big questions that guide this book. Let's jump in with some basic understanding of these questions.

An *aspiration* is a desire or ambition to achieve something. It is often a long-term and idealistic vision that a person or organization seeks to achieve in the future. Aspirations may be personal, professional, or related to social or environmental issues. Many of you reading this aspired to be in the position you currently hold. Many school districts aspire to great things when it comes to their staff and students. Unfortunately, these educational aspirations sometimes go unmet. The simple three-tier formula for understanding school district aspirations is to first think about expectations. If a district cannot deliver on basic expectations (of students, staff, parents, and community), there will never be an authentic conversation around aspirations. Once expectations have been met, however, we can then talk about desires. A *desire* is something we want to do. We desire to build a new stadium. We desire to offer an international baccalaureate. Once expectations and desires have been met, we can have a conversation about aspirations. If desire is something you wish to do, an aspiration is something you wish to be. In this regard, transformation can be either a desire or aspiration.

A *moral imperative* is a principle or belief that is essential or necessary for moral reasons. It is an obligation or duty that is considered to be morally right and just. For example, the belief that it is wrong to harm others is a moral imperative for many people. Many who are called into the highest levels of school leadership consider transformation to be a moral imperative.

A *goal* is a specific objective or target that a person or organization seeks to achieve. It is often a more concrete and measurable aim than an aspiration. Goals may be short term or long term and can be related to personal, professional, or organizational objectives. Goals are often used as a means of measuring progress toward a larger aspiration or vision.

In summary, an *aspiration* is a long-term vision or ambition, a *moral imperative* is a principle or belief that is considered essential for moral reasons, and a *goal* is a specific objective or target. While they are related, they differ in terms of their focus and level of specificity. Supporting transformational leadership is all of this. It is as big as you want to imagine, taking the visage of aspirations and moral imperatives. It can be as discrete as you would like, an example being launching one magnet school within your district.

To put it simply, this book will attempt to move transformation from conceptual to practical using just one framework. To be sure, this is not the only framework for transformational change, and by the end of the book, you will recognize you may have many of the elements to build your own framework. You will simply be shown a framework, given a description of why it works, be provided some examples along the way, and build a case that transformational leadership is indeed possible. This book will provide compelling evidence to convince you that you must have an agreed-upon framework to do the work of building supportive systemic structures that make for great schools.

To this end, this book is written for several audiences. First, if you are relatively new to your school leadership position (principal or superintendent), then it is likely you will not have a toolbox of working frameworks from which to draw on unless you had the rarefied experience of working with or for someone who made them explicit. Sadly, many leaders do not take the time to teach these frameworks with suspicion that part of the reason is we have not done a great job historically in education highlighting their value and teaching people to articulate the mental frameworks they use in planning or decision-making. The second type of reader is one who has been in a position for some time and has a sense of what works and what does not. The good news is that this means you probably have some frameworks, or pieces of frameworks at least, that are working well for you. You will be able to draw those frameworks to the surface and make them more explicit for yourself so you can teach others. The final audience is school board members. Board members play a critical and, sometimes, overlooked role in developing the capacity of the community to embrace real and lasting change. To be sure, many school boards intend to build the capacity of the community to embrace transformational change in their schools but are not provided a blueprint, template, or framework to make it happen. The specific framework detailed throughout this book is at the highest level of school governance . . . and school leadership.

GOVERNANCE OR LEADERSHIP

To be clear, school leadership and school governance are both essential components of effective school management, and both are critical for transformational change. However, they differ in their specific roles and responsibilities. School board members often find themselves walking a tight line between education leadership and governance and are often called upon to do both but not always at the same time.

First, both school leadership and school governance share the common goal of improving student outcomes. According to Leithwood and Riehl,[1] effective school leadership involves creating a vision for the school, promoting a positive school culture, and engaging in strategic planning to improve student learning. Similarly, school governance aims to ensure that schools are managed effectively, with a focus on improving student outcomes.[2] In this regard, we have leadership working at the vision, culture, and strategic planning, and governance is about the management of those efforts.

Second, it is important to note school leadership and school governance both involve decision-making. The framework you will read about in the coming chapters will require difficult (seemingly impossible) decisions. School leaders make decisions on a day-to-day basis, such as managing staff and resources, while school governance is concerned with making high-level strategic decisions, such as setting goals and priorities for the school.[3] Both school leaders and governance members need to use data and evidence to inform their decision-making and ensure that their actions align with the district's vision and goals. Sadly, this is where many school districts get hung up in the change process. It is normal human inclination to take an immensely dense and complex decision and break it down into more discrete and manageable complicated decisions. Although this may lead to easier decision-making, it runs the risk of losing the meta-perspective of the issue at hand. In *The Secret to Transformational Leadership*, I wrote extensively about the difference between complex and complicated decisions, so I won't belabor the point here except to say that complex decisions are inherently unknowable and complicated decisions have one right answer.

Despite these overlapping similarities, there are also significant differences between district leadership and district governance. Leadership refers to the day-to-day management of the district or school, including instructional leadership and the supervision of teachers and staff.[4] In contrast, governance refers to the broader system of oversight and accountability, typically involving a governing board or council responsible for setting policy and overseeing school management.[5] The framework described throughout this book will fall squarely in the governance role and specifically address policymaking.

Another key and important distinction between leadership and governance is the level of involvement in the school. School leaders are typically employed by the school and work within it, whereas school governance members are often external stakeholders, such as parents, community members, or government representatives.[6] This difference in perspective will influence the types of decisions made and the priorities set. The framework described throughout the book creates a forum whereby every governing board member has a chance to share their perspective on transformation. As stated previously, with complex decisions there is not just one right way to make change. This framework creates a platform for conversation, dialogue, and decision-making.

One final point about leadership and governance: They differ in their focus on different aspects of school management. School leadership is primarily concerned with instructional leadership, curriculum development, and the day-to-day management of the school.[7] In contrast, school governance is focused on the strategic planning, financial management, and accountability of the school.[8] Although both are important, the specific focus of each can differ depending on the school's context and needs. The framework described in the ensuing chapters will stay squarely in the governance lane and address strategic planning, financial management, and accountability (which I will call *quality control*).

While school leadership and school governance share some similarities, they are also distinct in their roles and responsibilities. Effective schools require both strong leadership and effective governance, and understanding the differences between the two can help schools to ensure that they have the right people in the right roles, working toward a common goal of improving student outcomes. This framework provides an opportunity for conversation between superintendent and school board about the transformative work we do in schools.

The purpose in writing this book is not a blueprint for how to do transformational leadership, but it does serve as a blueprint for creating a supportive systemic structures that allow for transformational leadership. Put simply, the framework I will provide is the governance blueprint that makes the leadership possible.

THE IMPACT OF GOOD GOVERNANCE

Excellence in school board governance refers to the effective leadership and management practices of a school board, including policymaking, oversight of educational programs, budgeting, and community engagement. Every state throughout the United States recognizes the outsized impact that great school governance can have on a school district, and much time, effort, and energy has been spent studying and disseminating what works. It is clear that great governance can lead to improved student achievement and outcomes because it provides a clear vision and direction for the school district, ensures accountability, and promotes collaboration among stakeholders. Note the use of the word *can* and not *always*. This is a point I will come back to at the end of this section. According to a study by the National School Boards Association (NSBA), effective school board governance can positively impact student achievement in several ways, including:

- Establishing clear expectations for student performance and holding educators accountable for results.
- Providing resources and support to educators to meet the needs of diverse learners.
- Promoting a positive school culture and climate that supports teaching and learning.
- Engaging families and community members in the education process.

A seminal work in this area is the Iowa Lighthouse Study, which examined the impact of effective school board governance on student achievement. The study found that school districts with strong governance practices had higher student achievement, better teacher retention, and greater community support than those with weak governance practices. Specifically, the study identified six characteristics of effective school board governance:

- Focusing on student achievement and outcomes.
- Providing resources and support for educators.
- Promoting a positive school culture and climate.
- Engaging families and community members.
- Being accountable for results.
- Planning for the future.

Other research has also supported the link between effective school board governance and improved student achievement. For example, a study by the Center for Public Education found that school districts with higher levels of student achievement had board members who were more knowledgeable about education policy and more actively involved in the governance process. Additionally, a meta-analysis of 27 studies by the NSBA found a positive correlation between effective school board governance and student achievement.

In summary, excellence in school board governance is critical to improving student achievement and outcomes. Effective governance practices can provide a clear vision for the school district, promote accountability, and foster collaboration among stakeholders. We can safely say effective governance is a necessary condition for student success, but is it sufficient? Is it enough? What is listed is part of the formula, but it is missing some key pieces. I urge you to go back to the preceding lists before reading further, and this time, instead of reading what is there, read into the negative space by asking what is missing. Make a list of these things before reading further.

Formulas are a great way to think about good governance. Imagine a number of constants or variables coming together in such a way that the formula equals student success. Of course, we would like to have everything, who wouldn't? However, we are much better served to simplify the formula into its most basic application. If you look at the two preceding lists, both contain something about the future or clear expectations. Both lists use the words *resources*, *support*, and *culture*. Engaging families is also important as is being accountable. Let's rearrange the formula and put it together like this:

$$\text{Clear outcomes} + \text{Support and Resources} + \text{Culture} + \text{Engaged Families} = \text{Student Success}$$

Oh, if it were that simple. Let's work on the formula from right to left to see what works, what does not work, and what might be missing. Engaged families is important, but it fails to account for the role that our communities play in the education of our students. The word *engage* carries a lot of baggage to be honest. We engage in war. We engage in a problem. Engagement is close to *buy-in*, and most people have no use for that word at all. These words should be buried forever when it comes to public education. So instead of *engaged families* let's use *community ownership*. We should no longer engage people around either a problem or solution but find ownership of that problem or solution. Next comes culture. That word is quite broad and can literally mean anything to anyone, thus relieving the word of having any real meaning at all. Simply adding *continuous improvement* to culture gives it concrete meaning. Next, we see *support and resources*. We cannot argue with that, but support and resources are descriptive terms that are all about capacity. Our capacity to do anything in life is a matter of priorities, resources, and processes. Let's use *capacity* because it has a bigger meaning than *support and resources*. This is also a lightbulb moment into what is missing from our understanding of great governance. What are we supporting exactly? The outcomes? That does not make intuitive sense. If we are applying resources to a problem, where and how do we know where to start? There is one big, missing variable from this equation, and it comes right after clear outcomes. The variable is *frameworks*. Now the formula reads like this:

Clear outcomes + Frameworks (for change) + Capacity + Continuous Improvement Culture + Community Ownership = Student Success

Although each of these variables will be touched on throughout the book, we will focus mostly on the notion of frameworks. Just one, well-designed framework can serve as a catalyst to the other variables in this formula of student success.

THE CASE FOR TRANSFORMATION

Why is transformation necessary? Transformational leadership and governance aims to inspire and motivate individuals and entire communities to reach their full potential by encouraging growth through a cycle of continuous improvement, creating a positive feeling about change, and fostering innovation and creativity. In education, transformational leadership is particularly important as we navigate the complex challenges of a rapidly changing educational landscape. There is undoubtedly a new level of urgency for transformational change in a postpandemic world.

First, we need innovation and creativity now more than ever. Much of how we do what we do has changed in schools, and the pandemic disrupted the traditional educational model. Educators and administrators are being forced to adapt to new ways of teaching and learning, and the rapid development of new tech tools are changing the nature of the classroom experience almost daily. In this environment, transformational leadership is necessary to encourage innovation and creativity, which are essential for creating effective and engaging learning experiences for students. As noted by Hill,[9] transformational leaders "encourage innovation and risk-taking, allowing for greater creativity in problem-solving and decision-making." Transformational leadership as described here simply cannot happen without the supportive systemic structures described in the coming chapters.

Transformation requires emotional intelligence. Teachers and administrators must be able to connect with students on an emotional level to build trust and rapport, which can be challenging in a virtual or hybrid learning environment. According to Goleman,[10] transformational leaders "create resonance with their followers through their emotional intelligence, which enables them to inspire and motivate others to achieve their full potential." This is also true from the governance lens and broadens beyond teachers, administrators, and students to include parents and community members. Emotional intelligence is the ability to recognize, understand, and regulate one's own emotions, as well as the emotions of others, to guide thought and behavior effectively.[11] It involves skills such as empathy, self-awareness, self-regulation, motivation, and social skills. Deep emotional empathy with a community is a critical step in building systemic structures to support transformational leadership.

The Need for Adaptability

In a post-pandemic educational environment, adaptability is more important than ever. Teachers and administrators must be able to quickly pivot to new teaching methods and technologies, which can be challenging for those who are resistant to change. Transformational leadership is necessary to foster a culture of adaptability and encourage individuals to embrace new ideas and approaches. As noted by Bass and Riggio,[12] transformational leaders "encourage their followers to be flexible and adaptable, and to continuously seek new opportunities for growth and development." Here, too, transformational leadership is an aspirational goal without a supportive structure that allows for adaptability. Far too often we ask teachers or campus leaders to change without providing the support to make that possible. It is quite literally setting ourselves up for failure.

Collaboration is essential in education because teachers, administrators, and students must work together to achieve common goals. This same notion of collaboration scales beyond the school walls and into the community if we are to be serious about real systemic transformation. This work cannot be done by teachers or students but falls squarely on the shoulders of the superintendent and school board in building the capacity within the community for transformative change. Transformational leadership is necessary to foster a culture of collaboration and create a sense of shared purpose and vision for as many as possible. According to Leithwood,[13] transformational leaders "foster a sense of community and shared responsibility, encouraging collaboration and teamwork."

The Need for Resilience

The pandemic was a stressful and challenging time for educators and students alike. In this environment, resilience is essential because individuals must be able to bounce back from setbacks and continue to persevere in the face of adversity. Transformational leadership is necessary to cultivate resilience and provide individuals with the support and resources they need to overcome challenges. According to Avolio and Yammarino,[14] transformational leaders "build the confidence and self-efficacy of their followers, enabling them to persevere in the face of adversity and bounce back from setbacks." Here, too, transformational leadership scales up and out into the community to build a community's resilience in the face of adversity. Have we created the language and structures that allow us to have these conversations with our community? The framework in this book creates an avenue for that conversation.

The Importance of Ethical Leadership

Ethical leadership is more important than ever. Teachers and administrators must make difficult decisions in the face of uncertainty, and they must do so with integrity and a commitment to doing what is right for their students. Transformational leadership is necessary to promote ethical behavior and create a culture of integrity and trust. We find this same responsibility for ethical governance. Transforming the supportive systemic structures that make for great schools requires the highest degree of governance ethics.

The Urgency for Change

Traditional models of teaching and learning have been disrupted, and educators and administrators must adapt to new ways of doing things. In this environment, transformational leadership is necessary to lead the way and drive change. As noted by Fullan,[15] transformational leaders "provide a clear vision for the future and inspire individuals to work together to achieve it." As stated previously, if we ask teachers and administrators to adapt to new ways of working, we owe it to them to provide a supportive systemic structure to make that work possible. Without this structure, we are asking them to build a castle on a foundation of sand.

The need for innovation, emotional intelligence, adaptability, collaboration, resilience, ethical leadership, and urgency for change has become more critical than ever. Leaders in education and those in governance roles must be able to inspire and motivate individuals to reach their full potential, create a positive work environment, and foster innovation and creativity. With transformational leadership, educators, administrators, and entire communities can navigate the complex challenges of a rapidly changing educational landscape and build a better future for students.

A FRAMEWORK OR THEORY OF ACTION

Thus far, you have been reading about transformational leadership and transformational governance. Let's level set our expectations and be clear what this book intends to do: It is a deep dive into the governance portion of transformation. Although the framework used encompasses both leadership and governance, we will be solely focused on the governance components through the remainder of the book. You are being given the full framework, and there exists a clear line of demarcation between transformative governance and transformative leadership. If you have been part of real transformative change, then you have likely seen parts of this framework in the past, but perhaps not presented in this format.

Frameworks and theories of action are important tools in understanding and guiding human behavior. Both frameworks and theories of action attempt to provide a structure for understanding how individuals and groups interact with their environment and make decisions. While *frameworks* and *theories of action* are often used interchangeably, they are distinct concepts with different purposes and applications. What follows is an attempt at a brief exploration of the similarities and differences.

A *framework* is a broad conceptual structure that provides a context for understanding a phenomenon or problem. Frameworks are typically descriptive in nature and aim to provide a way of categorizing and organizing data or information. Frameworks are often used in research to guide data collection and analysis and to help researchers identify patterns and relationships between variables. For example, the ecological systems theory provides a framework for understanding how individuals interact with their environment at multiple levels, from the individual level to the societal level.[16]

Theories of action, on the other hand, are prescriptive in nature and aim to explain how individuals or groups should act in a given situation. Theories of action are often based on a set of underlying assumptions or values and provide a road map for decision-making and problem-solving. For example, the theory of planned behavior posits that an individual's intention to engage in a behavior is influenced by their attitudes, subjective norms, and perceived behavioral control.[17] This theory provides a framework for understanding how to promote behavior change by targeting these three factors. When teaching this as part of university coursework, we talk about theories of action as a series of "If-then" statements. If I do (something), then I expect (something else) will occur. And if that happens, then something else will occur . . . and so on.

Despite their differences, frameworks and theories of action share some similarities. Both aim to provide a way of understanding human behavior and decision-making. Both are also used to guide research and practice in a variety of fields, including psychology, sociology, and education. Finally, both frameworks and theories of action are subject to revision and refinement as new evidence emerges. What is being shared is both a framework and a theory of action in this regard. This means that you can use it as a framework to review your existing transformational plan and identify strengths, weaknesses, opportunities, and threats. You could also use this as a theory of action should you want to start from scratch, so to speak, in building supportive systemic structures that allow for great schools. This tool can be used both inductively and deductively.

The primary difference between frameworks and theories of action is their purpose. *Frameworks* are descriptive in nature and provide a way of categorizing and organizing data or information. *Theories of action*, on the other hand, are prescriptive in nature and aim to guide decision-making and problem-solving. Additionally, frameworks are often broader in scope than theories of action because they provide a general structure for understanding a phenomenon or problem, and theories of action focus on a specific situation or context. As stated in the previous paragraph, the tool provided here is both a framework and theory of action. If you set out to describe what you currently have in place, this tool is a framework that allows you to better understand your own process and potentially identify both strengths and potential weaknesses. If you are setting out to do things differently, this tool becomes a theory of action that will guide you on the process for change.

Another key difference between frameworks and theories of action is their level of abstraction. Frameworks tend to be more abstract, providing a high-level conceptual structure for understanding a phenomenon or problem. If you choose to use this tool as a framework, it works in the abstract. I have been using this for many years with different school boards, and it has always been broad enough to capture every conversation. Theories of action, on the other hand, tend to be more concrete, providing a specific set of guidelines or steps for how to act in each situation. Should you use this tool as a theory of action, it is broad enough to give a starting point but will need much, much more detail before implementation.

Frameworks and theories of action are important tools in understanding and guiding human behavior. While they share some similarities, such as their use in guiding research and practice, they differ in their purpose and level of abstraction. Frameworks provide a broad conceptual structure for understanding a phenomenon or problem, whereas theories of action provide a specific set of guidelines for how to act in each situation. Both frameworks and theories of action are subject to revision and refinement as new evidence emerges. What is being provided to you is a tool that can serve as both a framework and a theory of action. It's all about your perspective!

MY INTEREST IN THIS TOPIC

I have been a school district superintendent for nearly two decades. I have served in three states. I have served rural districts and urban districts. I have served in economically disadvantaged communities and communities of high wealth. I have served in districts with little diversity and communities with large diversity where the minority is the majority. I have served through the good times, the bad, a pandemic, and a recovery. In every district I have been fascinated and inspired to chase innovation and transformation.

The inspiration for me in this work simplifies into a two-word question: What's possible? Since my teaching days, I have wondered what was possible in terms of growth. I wonder about the potential in every human I meet. I hope that I am the person who makes you and your life better because my genuine and authentic interest in your potential will eventually outweigh any self-doubt you may have. This inspiration does not just drive my work *in* the system, but it also drives my work *on* the system. I believe districts and schools are capable of innovation and transformation, but we often fall short of our goals. Worse, our best efforts might be realized for a year or two but then slowly begin to decay. I have endeavored to solve this problem since the onset of my career.

When you first start in any position, you tend to play by the rules as they are handed down to you. After some time though, you begin to realize you might just be playing a different game so you write new rules. I have been writing my rulebook for more than a decade and have learned what does work and what doesn't. To be sure, I do not purport to have all the answers, but I have been led by some good questions; this has helped me (and the school boards I have been privileged to work with) create supportive systemic structures that allow for great schools and transformational change.

THE LAYOUT

There are three parts to this book. The first part includes the first five chapters and will be an exploration of the tool and the tool will be presented mostly as a framework. Each of the chapters will add a new layer to the framework, and this is by design. Once finished with those five chapters, at which point you will have the five essential pieces of the framework in mind, you could put the book away, and never give it a second thought . . . although I hope you won't do that. These five chapters are what makes it possible to create supportive systemic structures that make for great transformational schools and districts. I hope that as you read these chapters you will have moments where you say to yourself, "Oh, I've done something like that before when . . . ." You will have a much deeper understanding of this tool if you have a concrete example in mind when real transformation took place in your school, your district, or your community that went well. It might also be helpful if you have an example where a transformational effort was less successful.

The second part of the book will pivot into a practical example of transformational change. Chapter 6 will provide background, an explanation of, and use cases in participatory budgeting (PB). Although the concept is not new, it is still mostly unfamiliar in the United States and certainly within the US education system. Chapter 7 will provide a case study on how PB was used in Victoria Independent School District as the largest example of PB by a school district in the history of the country. The tool will be applied as a theory of action in this second part of the book.

The final third of the book, chapters 8 and 9, will apply chapters 6 and 7 to the first five, thus bringing it all together. At this point, you will be able to read the tool both backward and forward. When reading the tool backward, it is best understood as a framework, and when reading the tool forward, it is best understood as a theory of action. Chapter 8 will be written for school and district administrators. Chapter 9 will be written for school board members with a focus on the governance implications to this work.

NOTES

1. K. Leithwood and C. Riehl, *What We Know about Successful School Leadership* (Philadelphia: Laboratory for Student Success, Temple University, 2005).

2. OECD (2013), "Synergies for Better Learning: An International Perspective on Evaluation and Assessment," *OECD Publishing*. https://doi.org/10.1787/9789264190658-en

3. T. Bush and L. Bell, *The Principles and Practice of Educational Management* (London: Paul Chapman, 2002).

4. Leithwood and Riehl, *What We Know about Successful School Leadership*.

5. Bush and Bell, *The Principles and Practice of Educational Management*.

6. OECD, "Synergies for Better Learning."

7. Leithwood and Riehl, *What We Know about Successful School Leadership*.

8. Bush and Bell, *The Principles and Practice of Educational Management*.

9. C. Hill, "Transformational Leadership in the Era of Change," *Journal of Business Strategy* 38, no. 1 (2017): 33.

10. D. Goleman, "Leadership That Gets Results," *Harvard Business Review* 78, no. 2 (2000): 78–90.

11. P. Salovey and J. D. Mayer, "Emotional Intelligence," *Imagination, Cognition and Personality* 9, no. 3 (1990): 185–211. doi: 10.2190/DUGG-P24E-52WK-6CDG

12. B. M. Bass and R. E. Riggio, *Transformational Leadership*, 2nd ed. (London: Psychology Press, 2006).

13. K. Leithwood, "Transformational School Leadership for Large-Scale Reform: Effects on Students, Teachers, and Their Classroom Practices," *School Effectiveness and School Improvement* 27, no. 1 (2016): 59.

14. B. J. Avolio and F. J. Yammarino, *Transformational and Charismatic Leadership: The Road Ahead* (Oxford: Oxford University Press, 2013), 44.

15. M. Fullan, *The Principal: Three Keys to Maximizing Impact* (New York: John Wiley & Sons. 2014), 12.

16. Urie Bronfenbrenner, *The Ecology of Human Development* (Cambridge, MA: Harvard University Press, 1979).

17. Icek Ajzen, "The Theory of Planned Behavior," *Organizational Behavior and Human Decision Processes* 50, no. 2 (1991): 179–211.

Chapter 1

Equitable Funding Structures

Funding
Establish equitable funding structures around student learning

Look at a district's budget and you will know what they value. When I was first earning my endorsement as a school superintendent many years ago, I had a professor who asked the class, "Should a good superintendent start with a vision and then build a budget or start with a budget and then set a vision?" Nearly every one of the students felt the answer was to start with vision. This crafty professor, after much debate, turned the conversation, and we collectively concluded that although you could set a vision first, the budget could easily undermine that vision as easily as it could support the vision. However, if you have a set budget, you can always build a vision around it. From a practical standpoint, our budget often drives our vision. When it comes to building great schools for kids, school transformation is necessary (as described in the introduction). Often, our lowest-performing and lowest-serving schools are in need of the greatest transformation. If we start with a vision to transform these schools, we have little hope of real success. The vision will quickly be undermined by the budget. We have set our vision on a foundation of sand. Let us understand that before we set a concrete vision for change, we must have a serious conversation about the budget.

Developing a systemic structure that supports transformation requires us to focus first on funding. When you think of your district budget, many things probably come to mind. Perhaps you think about the process and timeline. Perhaps you think about the funds and balances in each. It is possible you think first about local revenues, state revenues, and federal sources. Maybe your first thought is panic that we never have enough funding to support the work we want to do in our districts! You might think about expenses and immediately remember that across the nation, the average school district spends about 80 percent of their resources on staff (we are a people-intensive business). Everything described here is what is already in place. These are the things that got us where we are today. This is not the thinking that allows us to embrace and *support* transformational leadership. If there is an expectation that schools or a district must become transformational with some part of their program, how can this possibly happen without funding to support the initiative?

Throughout this book, we must remember the charge that we are building a foundation of granite that supports transformational change. This foundation is nothing without a serious conversation about funding. The question we need to ask is, "What are we funding, exactly?" I am quite certain the first thing that may come to mind is a program or support personnel, but I would encourage you to embrace this question, "What are we funding, exactly?" differently.

EQUITY IN STUDENT LEARNING: BEYOND ECONOMIC FACTORS TO HOLISTIC ACADEMIC SUPPORT

Equity in student learning is an essential goal for any education system. It is not only about ensuring equal access to resources but also about creating a level playing field for all students to reach their fullest potential. While economic equity plays a significant role in achieving this, equitable academic programming is just as crucial. In this section, you will be provided a brief overview of the concept of equity in student learning, focusing on providing students with challenging coursework and ensuring they have the tools and resources necessary for success. Additionally, examples of school districts recognized for their strides in promoting equity will be highlighted.

First, we must understand what *equity in student learning* means. *Equity in student learning* refers to providing all students with equal opportunities to succeed academically, regardless of their backgrounds, abilities, or circumstances.[1] This includes not only addressing financial disparities but also tailoring academic programs to meet the needs of diverse learners. Equity is achieved when all students have access to quality education that challenges them and prepares them for future success.

To foster equity in student learning, it is essential to provide students with challenging coursework that pushes them to think critically, solve complex problems, and develop essential skills.[2] At the same time, schools must ensure students have access to the tools and resources they need to succeed in these courses, including well-trained teachers, adequate learning materials, and support services. This is an important point and not one to simply gloss over. Providing all students with challenging coursework is one part of equity. The other part is the necessary supports and resources. Far too many school districts provide opportunities without supports or, worse, supports without opportunities.

Inclusive curriculum design is an essential aspect of achieving equity in academic programming. Schools must create curricula that are responsive to the diverse needs of students, allowing them to engage with the content in a meaningful way.[3] This can involve incorporating multiple perspectives, addressing cultural biases, and providing differentiated instruction to accommodate various learning styles.

An important aspect in this framework is professional development for teachers. Effective teachers play a critical role in promoting equity in student learning. Schools must invest in ongoing professional development for educators, ensuring they are equipped with the skills and knowledge to support diverse learners.⁴ This can involve training in culturally responsive teaching, differentiated instruction, and assessment strategies that promote equity.

Finally, support services for students are critical for their success. In addition to quality instruction, students who are given challenging coursework must have access to support services that help them succeed. This can include tutoring programs, academic advising, counseling services, and special education resources.⁵ By providing these supports, schools create an environment in which all students can thrive academically.

EXAMPLES OF SCHOOL DISTRICTS PROMOTING EQUITY

One example of a school district that has been recognized for making strides in equity for student learning is the San Francisco Unified School District (SFUSD). In 2014, SFUSD implemented an equity-focused policy aimed at reducing racial and socioeconomic disparities in student achievement. The policy included a comprehensive plan for addressing disparities in academic programming, teacher quality, and student discipline. SFUSD has also implemented a program called "Culturally Responsive Teaching and Leading" to help teachers better serve students from diverse backgrounds. SFUSD has also made significant strides by implementing a weighted student funding model that directs more resources to schools serving students with greater needs.⁶

Another school district making strides in equity for student learning is the Montgomery County Public Schools (MCPS) in Maryland. In 2015, MCPS adopted an Equity Accountability Model that includes a set of performance measures aimed at reducing disparities in student achievement across racial and socioeconomic groups. MCPS has also implemented a program called "Equity Initiatives Unit," which provides professional development opportunities for teachers and administrators focused on creating a more inclusive and equitable learning environment for all students.⁷

The Minneapolis Public Schools (MPS) provides another example of a district that has made significant progress in equity for student learning. In 2018, MPS launched an Equity Framework that includes a set of guidelines for ensuring that all students have access to high-quality educational opportunities. The framework includes strategies for reducing disparities in student achievement, improving teacher quality, and addressing issues related to school climate and culture. MPS has also implemented a program called "Equity Design Collaborative," which provides schools with tools and resources for creating more equitable learning environments.⁸

The Seattle Public Schools (SPS) is yet another district that has been recognized for its efforts to achieve equity in student learning. In 2017, SPS launched a strategic plan that includes a set of goals focused on reducing disparities in student achievement across racial and socioeconomic groups. The plan includes a variety of initiatives aimed at improving teacher quality, increasing access to advanced coursework, and providing additional support for struggling students.[9]

Finally, Austin Independent School District (AISD) in Texas has also been recognized for its efforts to achieve equity in student learning. In 2016,[10] AISD adopted an equity policy that includes a set of strategies for reducing disparities in student achievement across racial and socioeconomic groups. The policy includes a variety of initiatives aimed at improving teacher quality, increasing access to advanced coursework, and providing additional support for struggling students. AISD has also implemented a program called "Equity Action Teams," which provides schools with tools and resources for creating more inclusive and equitable learning environments.[11]

Efforts toward equitable outcomes are happening across the country in large and small schools alike. What we can learn from this is that achieving equity in student learning requires a collaborative effort among educators, policymakers, and community leaders to address the various factors that contribute to educational inequality. School districts like SFUSD, MCPS, MPS, SPS, and AISD have implemented policies and programs aimed at reducing disparities in student achievement and creating more inclusive and equitable learning environments. By focusing on the needs of all students and providing the tools and resources they need to succeed, these districts are helping to ensure that every student has an equal opportunity to achieve academic success. To be clear, having an equity outcome goal is important, but it is impossible to achieve without tools and resources. Tools and resources can only be available through budget and funding. This is why equitable funding structures must come first.

Several school districts have been recognized for their efforts in promoting equity in student learning. For example, the SFUSD has made significant strides by implementing a weighted student funding model that directs more resources to schools serving students with greater needs. Additionally, AISD has developed a comprehensive equity plan that includes teacher training, community engagement, and targeted support for marginalized student populations.

What I hope you take from this section is that equity in student learning refers to ensuring that every student, regardless of their background, has access to the same opportunities and resources that enable them to achieve academic success. While economic equity is a critical component of this concept, it is not the only factor. Creating equity in academic programming means ensuring that all students have access to the resources and support they need to succeed, including challenging coursework, personalized instruction, and academic enrichment programs. Achieving equity in student learning requires a collaborative effort among educators, policymakers, and community leaders to address the various factors that contribute to educational inequality. This includes providing equitable access to rigorous coursework, high-quality teaching, supportive learning environments, and appropriate instructional materials. In the context of creating equity in academic programming, it is essential to ensure that all students have access to the tools and resources they need to succeed, especially those who are taking more challenging coursework.

Equity in student learning goes beyond economic factors and requires a holistic approach to academic programming. By providing students with challenging coursework, access to resources, and targeted support, schools can create an environment where all learners have an equal opportunity to succeed. As demonstrated by the examples of SFUSD and AISD, it is possible to make significant strides toward achieving equity in education.

WHAT IS EQUITABLE FUNDING?

Equitable funding in education refers to the allocation of financial resources to ensure that all students, regardless of their race, socioeconomic status, or geographic location, have access to a high-quality education. It is a critical component of promoting educational equity overall, which seeks to provide all students with equal opportunities to succeed as described previously. Equitable funding aims to address the systemic disparities that exist in education, where students from historically marginalized groups often receive fewer resources and opportunities compared with their peers. In this section, we will examine equitable funding in education, the similarities between equality and equity, and the importance of equitable funding in promoting educational equity.

There are inherent systemic disparities built into every classroom, school, district, and state throughout the nation. These systemic disparities also exist at the federal level. We must first embrace this reality if we intend to do anything about it. At the micro (classroom) level, it can be found whenever we walk into a classroom and recognize different students have different needs. It is painful for every teacher and administrator to see those needs either unmet or partially met because of limited resources available. This is prevalent at the school and district level. Simply drive around any community with economic disparity, and it is immediately evident from an infrastructure lens where resources are often invested. Far too often in far too many school districts, the students with greater legitimate needs are apportioned pennies (if anything) above the average student.

Even at the federal level, these inequities exist. As an example of how this happens, take the Elementary and Secondary School Emergency Relief (ESSER) funds (post-COVID recovery funding), which were apportioned in such a way that lower income communities received greater funding as a percentage. This is a decidedly good thing and should close the equity gap when it comes to catching students up on any unfinished learning post-pandemic. Unfortunately, however, this is not the full story. The Associated Press[12] found that "school districts with the highest percentage of children living in poverty—the poorest 20 percent of districts in each state—were more than three times as likely as the wealthiest school districts to dedicate money to the construction of new buildings or classrooms. School districts with high levels of poverty were also more than twice as likely to include money for facilities repairs." The net effect was the students who most needed academic support did not get that support because districts were compelled to use the funding to handle basic infrastructure needs, which have largely gone unmet for decades. The inequities in the system run very deep.

Equitable funding differs from equal funding in that it recognizes not all students have the same needs. While equal funding may allocate the same amount of resources to every student or school district, equitable funding takes into account the unique needs of different student populations. Most state funding formulas account for some version of addressing unique needs for students as part of the formula. Debates for many years have taken place as to the weights within these formulas. For example, schools with a high proportion of students from low-income families may require additional resources, such as more teachers or support staff, to provide the necessary academic and social-emotional support. Equitable funding ensures that schools serving these students receive adequate funding to address their needs. Thinking about this as simply a "low-income" problem does not take a big enough frame, however. Students in career and technical education (CTE) programs also have programmatic needs that are often more expensive compared to their non-CTE peers. Students in special education should be part of the conversation. And this is also how we can begin to wrap our minds around transformational programming.

Imagine a pilot program, a magnet school, a public/private charter, a partnership school, or any other version of something that would be transformative within your system. The nature of the work that needs to be done in this space is such that we should immediately recognize there will be increased costs (e.g., curriculum, training, physical space needs, staff professional development). Without a commitment to and a conversation about equitable funding structures, no real (nor sustainable) innovation or transformation will occur. Of the numerous examples provided in the previous section, each of these came with a significant investment of staff, programming, curriculum, and so on.

Although equity and equality are sometimes used interchangeably, they have different meanings. *Equality* refers to the distribution of resources or opportunities in a way that is fair and impartial. In education, this means that all students are treated the same regardless of their background or circumstances. To build a systemic structure of transformational governance, all students (and staff) must have equal access. *Equity*, on the other hand, refers to the distribution of resources or opportunities in a way that is just and recognizes the different needs of different individuals or groups. In education, this means that resources are allocated based on the needs of each student to ensure that they have equal opportunities to succeed. This concept can be scaled to the school and district level as well.

In the United States, the education system is plagued by inequalities that prevent many students from receiving a high-quality education. One of the main factors contributing to these inequalities is the uneven distribution of funding among schools. Schools that serve disadvantaged communities often have fewer resources and lower-quality facilities than schools in more affluent areas. As a result, students from low-income families, students of color, and students with disabilities are disproportionately affected. In this chapter, we will explore the importance of creating equitable funding structures in education and the similarities between equality and equity.

Equitable funding in education, then, is a crucial component of creating a fair and just society. When schools are not adequately funded, students are unable to receive the education they need to succeed. This can lead to a range of negative outcomes, including lower academic achievement, higher dropout rates, and decreased opportunities for higher education and employment. Moreover, a lack of equitable funding structures can contribute to a cycle of poverty and inequality because students from disadvantaged communities are less likely to have the resources they need to break out of the cycle of poverty. This concept is scalable from national, state, and local structures.

As a result, creating equitable funding structures in education requires a multifaceted approach. It involves addressing issues of funding at the federal, state, and local levels. It also requires the involvement of all stakeholders, including educators, parents, policymakers, and community members. A framework seems like a good place to start!

Equitable funding is the foundational block in building supportive systemic structures for transformational leadership because it can help to reduce the inherent educational disparities, which ultimately lead to improved education outcomes. Put simply, when schools and students have access to the resources they need, they are more likely to succeed academically. This is true regardless of whether these students come from lower-income households.

Schools and students need access to the resources they need. A big takeaway from this section is that equity applies equally whether we are thinking about programs, wealth, race, or gender. Students from low-income families or minority backgrounds often face additional barriers to success, such as lack of access to technology or educational resources, thus compounding the problem. Equitable funding can help level the playing field and ensure that these students have access to the same opportunities as their peers.

STRATEGIES TOWARD EQUITABLE FUNDING

There are several different strategies used to achieve equitable funding in education. Each comes with potential strengths and pitfalls. In this section, you will be provided three strategies used to achieve equitable funding in education, with a brief analysis of each.

The first strategy is *weighted student funding*. This strategy allocates funding to schools based on the needs of individual students. Students with greater needs, such as those with disabilities or from low-income families, receive more funding. This approach ensures that resources are distributed fairly and can provide schools with the means to address the specific needs of their students. Many states have already designed some form of weighted student funding, and this same approach could be used at the district level, providing the balanced equity approach the district is trying to attain.

An analysis from the Education Commission of the States, "Can School Funding Reform Help Close the Achievement Gap" provides great insight in the positives and negatives within this approach.[13] The merits of weighted student funding ensures that funding is distributed fairly and is tailored to the needs of individual students. This approach can lead to increased equity in educational opportunities and can help to reduce achievement gaps between different student groups. The pitfall in this approach is that it can create a lack of predictability in funding for schools because the amount of funding each school receives can fluctuate depending on the needs of individual students. This approach can also lead to unintended consequences, such as schools competing for students with fewer needs to receive more funding.

A second strategy involves *statewide funding formulas*. This approach involves establishing a statewide formula for distributing funding to schools based on various factors, such as student enrollment, teacher salaries, and school size. This strategy aims to ensure that all schools receive a fair and equitable share of funding. Again, this strategy can be scaled to a district level, but this is rarely attempted for the reasons described below.

From the National Conference of State Legislatures, we learn some of benefits and consequences of this approach. The merits of statewide funding formulas are that it can help to reduce disparities in funding across schools and can ensure that schools with greater needs receive additional resources. This approach can also increase transparency and accountability in the funding process. The pitfalls include that it can be difficult to implement and may not take into account the unique needs of individual schools and students. This approach can also result in some schools receiving less funding than they need, particularly if they are located in areas with high costs of living.[14]

As a final strategy, there is always *school finance litigation*. This approach involves taking legal action to challenge the constitutionality of state funding systems that result in disparities in funding across schools. This strategy has been used successfully in several states to increase funding for schools with greater needs.[15] This is obviously not a strategy that could be used at the local level.

From this litigation, we learn that this approach can be an effective way to bring attention to the issue of inequitable funding in education and can result in increased funding for schools with greater needs. This approach can also help to ensure that all students have access to a quality education. The pitfalls in school finance litigation are that it is a lengthy and costly process, and the outcomes are not always guaranteed. This approach can also lead to political backlash and can create tension between school districts and state policymakers.

AN EQUITABLE FUNDING PLAN

The simple place to start is with just one question: How much are we willing to invest in transformation? There are many good ways to think about this, and I think there are some bad ways to think about this. Good ways to think about this include a lump sum, a per-school amount, a per-student amount, or a per-staff amount. Each of these is different, of course, and each can be an extremely valuable perspective. Stop for a moment and ask yourself how much per student would our district be willing to invest to build innovative programming at historically low-performing campuses in need of improvement? You will likely grossly mistake the scaling impact of decisions at the student level with decisions at the school or district level. A small amount at the per-student level can lead to a large amount when compounded.

The wrong way to approach this conversation is to ask, "What do we hope to accomplish?" This is essentially putting the vision before the budget. Every district in this country is designed to get exactly what we are currently getting. Creating a new vision and then hoping to fund that vision is asking far too much from the system and its ability to change. This is the single biggest reason most transformation and innovation fails in school districts.

School innovation must take place *outside* the boundaries of the traditional school setting to provide more diverse and authentic learning experiences for students. In his book *What Schools Could Be*, Ted Dintersmith argues that traditional schooling methods do not adequately prepare students for the rapidly changing world and that innovation is necessary to provide more meaningful and relevant learning opportunities.[16] Dintersmith studied several districts that have made strides in innovation and transformation and found that each of these districts committed to building the program outside of the franchise operation that is the traditional school district.

Furthermore, innovation in education is enhanced through collaboration with partnerships and organizations, which can provide students with greater opportunities in programming, access to programming, or support. This can also help bridge the gap between what we know and what we do not yet know.

Innovation and transformation in education should take place outside the traditional school setting to provide students with diverse and authentic learning experiences, which can better prepare them for the rapidly changing world. This can involve experiential learning, the use of technology, and collaboration with industry professionals and organizations.

If the research is clear (and it is) that innovation and transformation must happen in a way that is somehow apart from the franchise model of the district, it simply is not possible without having the first conversation around equitable funding structures and what resources will be made available. Once these fundamental budget questions have been answered, you will have an idea of the funds available, and thus, questions like, is this a program, a pilot, a curriculum, or all, finally become relevant. Other questions begin to surface as well: With whom? What group of students? What is the demographic makeup of that population?

Regardless of whether this is a pilot program in just one school, a full school-wide program at just a few campuses, or full-scale district change, the scope of the funding structures will determine the scope of the projects to be developed.

A PRACTICAL EXAMPLE

Here is how the math might work. If a typical elementary campus has approximately five hundred students, how much are we willing to carve out of our budget per student to develop an innovative program? Perhaps $100 per student. The math is easy on this (which is why we're starting here), $50,000. That is probably not enough to cover the costs of one additional teacher (salary and benefits) but would be enough to cover the costs of a program. You can imagine the sorts of things you can do with $50,000 per campus.

But there is a flaw in the example. We are robbing from Peter to pay Paul, so to speak. We are taking money out of a campus that needs support to find "new money" to support that same campus. At the end, it is a wash. The district is investing nothing new in the campus at all. This is the opposite of equity in funding. Sadly, this is far too commonplace around the county. We have countless heroic principals and teachers who want to do amazing things with kids, and they receive the following response: "If you can find it in your budget." To be sure, there are districts that think differently, but this is sadly not the norm.

Let's tackle the first example again and think differently. Let's start with the same idea of $100 per student (I am using $100 because the math is easier and not because this is a good amount). Let's also assume the district has an enrollment of about seven thousand students pre-K–12, and of that body, there are about four thousand students of elementary age. If we are focused on just one campus at the elementary, we want to be mindful of the equity implications of taking money from high schools or middle schools to support the elementary school. It might be a good investment, but it could also be a really bad investment. These are the conversations to be had in budget planning and budget workshop cycles. The $100 per student applied to the elementary student population now creates a funding stream of $400,000. This is a radically different conversation from the first.

Furthermore, and, this is important, it addresses equity by holding back the same amount for every student (equal distribution of costs) to create additional monies for the innovation site. The innovation site has more available dollars per student than the remaining campuses throughout the district. It becomes the work of the district budgeting office and campus administration to then design a plan that would bring down the costs of operations by $100 per student.

The beautiful part of thinking this way is how freeing the conversation becomes. One of the biggest obstacles we face in education is constraining variables. One successful tip that savvy school leaders of innovation learn is to take constraining variables and turn those into enabling variables. If we start on the wrong foot with a vision and look to the budget, then the budget becomes the constraining variable. If we start with the budget, then begin thinking of programs, the budget becomes an enabling variable.

As a brief aside, we have countless constraining variables in education that are utterly useless. The high school schedule is a great example. Class size per teacher is another, as are school start and end times. Available technology is another still. This list is endless. In my experience, nearly all can be flipped from constraining to enabling with the right team and enough motivation.

A few words about the amount. Don't get hung up on $100. For some districts, this may not seem like a stretch. For others, this amount may be out of the question. There is a give and take to any budget preparation calendar, and the guiding question should be "what's possible?" If $50 per student is the maximum amount and there are just three thousand students in the district, then we have $75,000 in equitable funding to support our elementary campaign ($50 multiplied by 1,500 elementary students).

These conversations can scale from elementary to secondary just as easily. The balance between equality of offerings and equity of opportunity is a dance we all must learn. Making a commitment to address funding as a first step is critical for that conversation.

Must the district create its own funding stream, you ask? No, of course not. You have no doubt heard of or have participated in a grant-funded program at some point in your service. Maybe the grant funded a program or innovation. Typically, those funds are applied directly, and this has the same impact as what has been described. The benefits to grants are that new monies flow into the district. The negative is that those grants eventually end and without the equitable funding plan, so does the program.

The first grant conversation to be had is whether new funding grants or existing grants are being looked for. If new funding grants is the answer, there are some follow-up questions, including competitive funding or flat funded? Corporate, foundation, state, or other? Who will write the grant? What is the plan if unsuccessful? If you choose to look at existing grants, the first question is which ones (federal or state)? After that, what level of flexibility does the district have within those grants? These are all detailed and complicated questions, and these answers should be brought from administration to the board for consideration. In *The Secret to Transformational Leadership*, we learn about differentiating between complex and complicated problems. Complicated problems are the work of administration because they require technical expertise. Complex problems are the work of the board because they are inherently unknowable.

These conversations can scale from elementary to secondary just as easily. The balance between equality of offerings and equity of opportunity is a dance we all must learn. Making a commitment to address funding as a first step is critical for that conversation.

IMPACT

If you were asked what is the greatest impact in creating an equitable funding structure, what would your answer be? Many of you are likely to immediately start thinking about kids, teachers, and programs. You may think of school sites in need of support. Perhaps you picture smiling students and parents who are grateful for these additional opportunities. Those images may indeed play out, but sometimes transformation just does not work. It is, after all, innovation, and innovation by its definition often fails. There is a chance for success, to be sure, but there is also risk of failure. Further, these images of students, staff, and parents are still years away. Figure a year of planning, a year or two of deployment, scaling, and then impact. It may be as much as three or four years before any impact is realized. My advice would be to not use these imagines as the rationale for creating an equitable funding structure. The equitable funding structure we are describing will not be lovingly embraced by all within your community. There will be some who think certain campuses are more deserving than others. There will be some who see this as "loss" for them for the "benefit" of others. If we try to sell our vision of smiling happy children (that won't happen for four years) while instituting an equitable funding structure, we are asking for trouble. The payoff takes too long, and it is not guaranteed. So, if not smiling happy children and staff, what should we be talking about when it comes to impact?

Transparency. District budgeting processes are insanely complicated. We have more legal requirements than nearly any business you can imagine. We have teams of experts that help advise the district on anything to bonds, audits, procurement, financial forecasting, and more. Often, it takes months and months of hard work by countless individuals to bring forward a budget to the school board, and the board gets a few meetings to understand, ask questions, give insight where needed, and approve. This is some of the hardest work a board does. They cannot possibly have all the information they need, must trust the experts, and are ultimately accountable to the community. It is like having no real authority but with total responsibility.

By having an equitable funding structure conversation at the onset of the budget cycle in a public forum, we are signaling to our community that we intend real change. It forces us to prioritize some campuses over others. It forces us to have a conversation about what is best for all students. All of this takes place on a public stage. As a concrete example, about halfway through the pandemic (if there was a halfway point), we began noticing tremendous needs with many of our students around mental well-being. We took this conversation forward to our board and had it publicly over the course of several months. We came up with a number we wanted to invest at the campus level and then set out to find that funding within our system. What did we do? We hired social emotional behavior specialists (SEBSs) at our campuses with the greatest needs. The program proved to be a tremendous success so we shifted our thinking from equity to equality. We targeted new campuses and added additional staff. What started as school or campus transformation has become district transformation.

What other impact will we notice immediately? Clarity. We can be much clearer about the exact dollar amount we are creating. With that clarity, we can be much more specific about what we plan to do with this funding. Imagine the reverse for a moment. Often we have an idea, like a project-based learning school for instance, and then go out and write a grant for the school. What level of clarity do you have with this plan? Very little, of course. We know there is a big pile of cash that is available for one campus if the grant is successful, and there are usually some but limited details on what that grant will actually support.

In conclusion, while the images of smiling students and parents may be the ultimate goal of creating an equitable funding structure, it should not be the main rationale used to sell this idea to the community. Instead, transparency and clarity should be the focus when discussing the impact of an equitable funding structure. By having conversations about equity in a public forum, we can signal to the community that we are committed to real change and prioritize the needs of all students. This clarity allows us to be specific about the exact dollar amount we are creating and what we plan to do with this funding. This transparency can lead to district transformation, as was the case with hiring SEBSs for campuses in need. While there is a risk of failure in innovation, prioritizing transparency and clarity in creating an equitable funding structure is a guaranteed step in the right direction. By starting with an equitable funding conversation at the onset, we are providing transparency and clarity for our community. We are signaling our intentions publicly. We are inviting our public into the conversation. Equitable funding creates a path for productive conversations about real change. These things cannot be taken for granted because they are the foundational structure we will continue to build in the following chapters.

Before revealing the next step that follows establish equitable funding structures around student learning, what do you think comes next? If the funding is in place, and we have some sense of what we will be taking on, there are many next steps in the path. Sometimes these next steps work and sometimes they don't. I believe the next step is both natural and necessary. It is natural because it is logical. If we know what funds we have and what we plan to do with those funds, then there is just one logical next step. This next step is necessary, because without it, the rest of the foundation falls apart.

NOTES

1. Darling-Hammond, *The Flat World and Education.*
2. Boser and Baffour, "Isolated and Segregated."
3. Gay, *Culturally Responsive Teaching.*

4. Ingersoll and Strong, "The Impact of Induction and Mentoring Programs for Beginning Teachers."

5. Roza, "Funding Student-Centered Education Policy."

6. San Francisco Unified School District, "Culturally Responsive Teaching and Leading."

7. Montgomery County Public Schools, "Equity Initiatives."

8. Minneapolis Public Schools, "Equity Framework."

9. Seattle Public Schools, "Our Strategic Plan."

10. Austin Independent School District, "Equity Policy."

11. Austin Independent School District, "Austin ISD Equity Action Plan."

12. Education Week, "Poorer Districts Were More Likely to Use COVID Relief Money to Repair Buildings."

13. Education Commission of the States, "Can School Funding Reform Help Close the Achievement Gap?"

14. National Conference of State Legislatures, "School Funding 101."

15. Education Commission of the States, "School Finance Litigation: An Overview."

16. Dintersmith, *What Schools Could Be*.

Chapter 2

Quality Assurance and a Cadence of Accountability

Perhaps you noted in the Introduction that accountability does not fall into our formula for student success although it was mentioned in the research. This by design because this term has become widely misunderstood and misapplied in the education space. Overuse of the word for nearly anything that can be measured in education for the past two decades has led to a lot of confusion and simplification at the same time. Further, when the only tool you have is a hammer, it's funny how everything starts to look like a nail. Accountability is largely misapplied in education because far too many school boards, superintendents, state officials, and communities see accountability as a hammer. These people are quick to use accountability as a tool for judgment and not improvement. This is the antithesis of continuous improvement culture. Let us be clear, if we add *accountability* to the formula, both it and the phrase "continuous improvement culture" disappear. The reason is simple. Accountability begets judgment and judgment begets compliance (not improvement).[1] This problem plagues high-performing and low-performing schools alike throughout the country. It is important to ensure this chapter is not characterized as being opposed to accountability. We should be opposed to using words that have deleterious impact on our goals. Accountability has become one of these words. Since no self-respecting administrator or board member would be opposed to measuring outcomes and sharing those results publicly, instead of *accountability*, let us use the phrase *quality assurance*.

Quality assurance is the second stage in our work toward building supportive systemic structures that make for great schools. Quality assurance is a much more scalable term than accountability. Where accountability tends to be narrow, quality control serves the purpose of being broad. We can expand our conversation to effective delivery of services, staff preparation and professional development, or any number of other areas. Quality assurance can be narrow, however, focused on the perspective of the student desk and student day, for example.

A QUICK HISTORY OF ACCOUNTABILITY?

A Nation at Risk, a report published by the National Commission on Excellence in Education in 1983, highlighted the alarming state of American education.[2] The report identified several key issues such as the low achievement of students, the inadequacy of teaching standards, and the lack of accountability measures in the education system. In response to these findings, several states began to implement accountability measures to improve student achievement. Many scholars recognize the publishing of this report as a pivotal moment in education. This was the first time the US government told the public there was a problem with public education. Communities, parents, and legislators responded with aplomb; the problem was teachers and curriculum. Over the ensuing decades, the accountability movement began to grow. Measuring student achievement became the only way we could measure student success. Measuring that success allowed us to look back and make inferences about the quality of the teacher or quality of the school. This logic is absurd. Simply imagine a patient in a doctor's office with severe health issues. When the patient returns three weeks later, they are worse. Educational accountability would put the burden solely on the physician and pay no attention to any underlying factors about the patient (say, for instance, they were 112 years old). In everyday life, we recognize people show up differently in their space and in our world. Educational accountability did not allow for us to make these distinctions, however.

The No Child Left Behind (NCLB) act, signed into law in 2002, was a significant milestone in the history of school accountability in the United States. The law required states to establish a system of accountability that would measure student progress in reading and math. Schools that failed to meet adequate yearly progress (AYP) targets were subject to sanctions, including funding cuts and restructuring.[3] The law was intended to improve student achievement and close the achievement gap between disadvantaged and non-disadvantaged students. It did neither. It's important to note that schools not making AYP were subject to "transformational" efforts. Nearly all of these efforts fell flat, however. The inherent problem is in sequencing. Putting accountability before equitable funding guarantees failure. Furthermore, funding wasn't even addressed in the NCLB act.

Although in the ten years following the signing of NCLB, when adjusted for inflation, we saw increases in federal education funding from 2002 to 2012; data from the National Center for Education Statistics found that although federal funding did increase over this period, it did not necessarily keep up with inflation or with the increasing demands placed on schools by the act.[4] Some education advocates argued that the law's requirements were underfunded, particularly for schools serving low-income students. This takes us back to the first element in building supportive structures for transformation, equitable funding mechanisms.

Increasingly, the NCLB act was criticized for its emphasis on high-stakes testing, which led to a narrowing of the curriculum and a focus on test preparation rather than authentic learning. Furthermore, the law's reliance on AYP targets was criticized for being too simplistic and not accounting for the complexity of student achievement. As a result, in 2015, the Every Student Succeeds Act (ESSA) replaced NCLB, giving states more flexibility in developing their accountability systems.[5] Unfortunately, some states took more progressive approaches than others and what remains is a hodgepodge of mostly antiquated systems that do not allow for any reasonable state-to-state comparison as it relates to either student learning or student growth. As it stands currently, all states use a different state accountability system to measure student achievement. These systems vary widely in their approach, with some states placing more emphasis on high-stakes testing than others. For example, Florida's accountability system, which is based largely on high-stakes testing, has been widely criticized for its negative effects on teaching and learning. In contrast, states like Massachusetts have developed more holistic accountability systems that take into account factors such as school climate, teacher quality, and student engagement.

And how does all of this relate to our performance internationally? Comparing student achievement results nationally with Trends in International Mathematics and Science Study (TIMMS) data from other countries highlights the need for continued improvement in the US education system. In the 2019 TIMMS report, the United States ranked eleventh in fourth-grade math and eighth in fourth-grade science among participating countries.[6] While these results are an improvement from previous years, they still lag behind other countries, such as Singapore and Japan, which consistently rank at the top of the TIMMS rankings.

The history of school accountability in the United States has been marked by a shift from a lack of accountability measures to an overemphasis on high-stakes testing and finally the opportunity to create a more balanced approach that takes into account multiple measures of student achievement. While there is still room for improvement in state accountability systems, the implementation of the ESSA has allowed for greater flexibility (although this flexibility has not always been put into place) and innovation in these systems. However, the United States still lags behind other countries in student achievement, highlighting the need for continued improvement in the educational accountability system.

WHAT WORKS IN ACCOUNTABILITY

We are stuck in a bit of a quandary. We know accountability is one piece of the puzzle in creating a quality education, but it doesn't guarantee success. It is natural then to wonder what is going right when accountability does work and can we design a system around what works. We know accountability should ensure that students, parents, and educators have a clear understanding of what is expected, how performance will be measured, and what consequences will be imposed. Two types of accountability systems that show great promise are community-based accountability and benefits-based accountability. In this section, I will briefly examine both systems, compare them, and argue that community-based accountability is the superior system for measuring student outcomes in education.

Community-based accountability is a bottom-up approach to accountability that emphasizes local control, community engagement (more on this word in the next chapter), and shared decision-making. It places responsibility for student success on and in the community rather than on external authorities. Community-based accountability systems involve a diverse group of stakeholders, including parents, teachers, community leaders, and local businesses. This system is grounded in the belief that education is a collaborative effort and that the community should play a role in shaping education policy.

Benefits-based accountability is often a top-down approach to accountability that emphasizes external standards, centralized decision-making, and punitive measures. It places responsibility for student success on external authorities, such as the government or school board. Benefits-based accountability systems rely on standardized tests and other quantitative measures to evaluate student performance. The goal of this system is to improve student outcomes by setting clear expectations, providing incentives, and imposing consequences for failure.

John Tanner, in his far-reaching work on accountability, argues that community-based accountability is a better system for measuring student outcomes in education. He argues that community-based accountability systems are more effective because they are more responsive to the needs of the local community. Tanner contends that benefits-based accountability systems are too rigid, too focused on quantitative measures, and too reliant on external authorities. Tanner further argues that community-based accountability systems are more effective because they involve a wider range of stakeholders in decision-making. This system ensures that educators, parents, and community leaders have a voice in shaping education policy. Tanner provides insight into the fact that benefits-based accountability systems are too focused on external authorities, which can lead to a disconnect between decision makers and those affected by their decisions. Tanner also shows that community-based accountability systems are more effective because they are more flexible. This system allows educators to tailor instruction to the needs of individual students and respond quickly to changing circumstances. Tanner argues that benefits-based accountability systems are too rigid and do not allow for individualized instruction or responsiveness to local needs.[7]

In recent years, various accountability models have emerged globally, some of which have been successful in improving student achievement and narrowing the achievement gap. Because of the success with community-based accountability, some states are designing and/or implementing community-based accountability systems. The state systems I will describe use frameworks designed to measure the effectiveness of schools in achieving their educational goals. Such models are crucial for ensuring that schools provide quality education and meet the expectations of stakeholders, including students, parents, educators, and policymakers.

One example of a state designed community-based accountability system is the California School Dashboard. The California School Dashboard is a community-based accountability system that provides a comprehensive picture of school performance using multiple measures. The system includes academic indicators such as test scores, graduation rates, and college readiness, as well as other measures such as suspension rates, attendance, and parent engagement. The system is designed to involve community members, including parents, students, and educators, in the assessment process and to provide a transparent and accessible tool for evaluating school performance.[8]

Another example of a state designed system is the Oregon Community-Based Accountability System: The Oregon Community-Based Accountability System is a locally driven approach to school accountability that emphasizes the use of multiple measures of school performance, including academic measures, as well as measures of school climate, parent engagement, and student voice.[9] The system is designed to be flexible and adaptable to the unique needs of each community and to provide a more comprehensive picture of school performance than traditional accountability systems.

Often, however, community-based accountability systems are being implemented at the local level and without state sanctioned support, often leaving communities confused when they receive state accountability reports that are different from the local community-based accountability system. When building a supportive systemic structure that allows for great schools, how we think about accountability will have an outsized impact on our success.

Community-based accountability is a superior system for measuring student outcomes in education. This system is more responsive to local needs, involves a wider range of stakeholders in decision-making, and is more flexible than benefits-based accountability. Community-based accountability systems are currently being developed in many states and have been shown to be effective in improving student outcomes.

QUALITY CONTROL OR QUALITY ASSURANCE

Because community-based accountability allows us to think more expansively than just test scores, we are able to open the door for a broader range of conversations about accountability. Some measures will be strictly internal (ensuring that students have access to devices during a lesson, for instance) and other measures may be externally focused (the frequency of web pages that do not contain active links on the district website). Both of these are matters of quality of experience, and although one could argue each of these examples may have a marginal impact on student performance, we would never dream of building them into a community-based accountability structure.

Quality control is an essential concept that has been applied in various sectors of the economy, including education in some instances. Quality control refers to the measures that are put in place to ensure that the products or services offered by an organization meet or exceed the expectations of the customers. Hopefully, you can see how an equitable funding structure begs for quality control standards to ensure the expectations can meet the outcomes.

Quality control has a long history dating back to the 1920s when it was first applied in the manufacturing sector.[10] The concept was developed by a statistician named Walter Shewhart, who was working for the Bell Telephone Laboratories. Shewhart came up with the idea of using statistical methods to monitor the production process and detect any deviations from the expected standards. He introduced the concept of control charts, which enabled the engineers to track the variations in the manufacturing process and make the necessary adjustments to improve the quality of the products.

Later, in the 1940s, another scholar, W. Edwards Deming, expanded on Shewhart's ideas and applied them to post-World War II Japanese industry. Deming is considered the father of the modern quality control movement. He introduced the concept of total quality management (TQM), which focuses on continuous improvement and involves all employees in the quality improvement process.[11]

In the field of education, quality control is also being used to ensure that the education products and services meet the desired quality standards. For instance, accreditation agencies such as the Council for Higher Education Accreditation (CHEA)[12] and the Accrediting Commission for Schools,[13] Western Association of Schools and Colleges (WASC) set standards and guidelines for the evaluation of educational programs and institutions. The standards cover areas such as curriculum, faculty, student support services, and institutional resources. On a micro scale, quality control in education can be seen in the assessment of individual students' academic performance. Teachers use various assessment tools such as exams, quizzes, and assignments to monitor students' academic progress and identify areas that need improvement. They also use rubrics and other assessment criteria to ensure that the assessments are valid and reliable.

Quality control and quality assurance are two terms that are often used interchangeably, but they refer to different concepts in the field of quality management. It is important to understand the similarities and differences between quality control and quality assurance. Some examples of each will be provided as well because having a good understanding is key to applying the framework with success.

As described, quality control refers to the measures that are put in place to ensure that the products or services offered by an organization meet or exceed the desired quality standards. The primary focus of is to detect and correct defects or errors in the products or services before they reach the customers. Quality control is a reactive approach to quality management and is applied after the production process is completed. This is an important aspect of quality control, the fact that it comes after. Examples of quality control include inspection of products, testing, and validation.

On the other hand, quality assurance refers to the planned and systematic activities that are put in place to ensure that the products or services offered by an organization meet the desired quality standards. The primary focus of quality assurance is to prevent defects or errors in the products or services before they occur. Quality assurance is a proactive approach to quality management and is applied during the production process. Examples of quality assurance include the development and implementation of quality standards, training of employees, and process improvement.

Despite their differences, quality control and quality assurance share some similarities. First, both aim to ensure that the products or services offered by an organization meet or exceed the desired quality standards. Second, both involve the use of quality metrics to evaluate the effectiveness of the quality management system. Finally, both require the involvement of all stakeholders in the quality improvement process.

The primary difference between quality control and quality assurance is the time at which they are applied. Control is applied after the production process is completed, and assurance is applied during the production process (although these phrases come from industry, they are applicable to education). Another difference is their approach to quality management. Quality control is a reactive approach that focuses on detecting and correcting defects or errors in the products or services, whereas quality assurance is a proactive approach that focuses on preventing defects or errors in the products or services. Additionally, quality control involves inspection and testing of outcomes or services, and quality assurance involves the development and implementation of quality standards and training.

Examples of quality control include inspection of products, testing, and validation. For instance, a manufacturer may conduct an inspection of the finished products to detect any defects or errors before they are shipped to the customers. In the service industry, a hotel may conduct a validation test on the room service to ensure that the food quality meets the desired standards. In education, we can assess the cleanliness of a lunchroom.

Examples of quality assurance include the development and implementation of quality standards, training of employees, and process improvement. For instance, a school district may develop a "profile of a graduate" (or "portrait of a graduate"), as many have, that meets the desired quality standards. Another example would be to provide training to employees to ensure that they understand and adhere to the board policies and administrative regulations.

One example of a school district in the United States that is using a quality assurance framework as part of a district improvement strategy is the Baltimore City Public Schools (BCPS) in Maryland. BCPS has adopted the Quality Assurance Review (QAR) process, which is a comprehensive approach to ensuring high-quality educational programs and services. The QAR process includes a review of district-wide policies and procedures, school-level practices, and instructional programs. The process also involves the collection and analysis of data to inform decision-making and continuous improvement.[14]

According to a report by the National Center for Education Evaluation and Regional Assistance, BCPS has been using the QAR process since 2010 as part of its district improvement strategy.[15] The report found that the QAR process has helped BCPS to identify areas of strength and weakness in its educational programs and services and to develop targeted improvement plans. Additionally, the QAR process has facilitated the sharing of best practices across the district and has improved communication and collaboration among district and school leaders.

Quality control and quality assurance are two essential concepts in the field of quality management, and understanding both will help us decide which is more appropriate to our framework. Quality control is a leadership and management function. Quality assurance is a governance and leadership function. Building a supportive systemic structure for transformation requires a governance mindset and, thus, a more expansive view, and this can only happen through quality assurance.

QUALITY ASSURANCE AS A GOVERNANCE FUNCTION

Quality assurance in business and board governance in education share some overlap. As concepts, both aim to ensure that the outcomes or services offered by an organization meet the desired quality standards. In this section, a rationale for the practical application of quality assurance in education will be provided, and the case will be made that school boards, along with superintendents, should create quality assurance frameworks. Finally, an analysis of whether it is more or less important to do this during times of change will be provided.

Quality assurance in business involves the planned and systematic activities that are put in place to ensure that the products or services offered by an organization meet the desired quality standards. Similarly, board governance in education involves the planned and systematic activities that are put in place to ensure that the educational programs and services offered by an organization meet the desired quality standards and outcomes. Both concepts require a focus on the development and implementation of policies and procedures, the collection and analysis of data, and the continuous improvement of processes. You will recall a culture of continuous improvement was one of the things mentioned in the Introduction that is an antecedent for successful student outcomes.

The practical application of quality assurance in education involves the development and implementation of quality standards, training of staff, the collection and analysis of data, and the continuous improvement of educational programs and services. As previously described, one example of a quality assurance framework in education is the QAR process used by BCPS. The QAR process involves a review of district-wide policies and procedures, school-level practices, and instructional programs. The process also involves the collection and analysis of data to inform decision-making and continuous improvement.

School boards, along with superintendents, should endeavor to create quality assurance frameworks to ensure the educational programs and services offered by their organization meet the desired quality standards of their community. Quality standards of their community is how and why community-based accountability reenters the picture. Quality assurance frameworks provide a systematic approach to ensuring quality and facilitate continuous improvement. By implementing quality assurance frameworks, school boards can ensure their educational programs and services are aligned with the mission and vision of the organization.

A question that surfaces regularly is whether quality assurance frameworks are more or less important during times of rapid change. During times of change, such as changes in leadership or significant policy changes, you would be right to assume it is more important than ever to have quality assurance frameworks in place. Quality assurance frameworks provide a stable foundation for continuous improvement, especially in times of change. These frameworks can help to ensure that new policies and procedures are implemented effectively and that staff members are adequately trained and supported to implement these changes.

Niu[16] discusses the different approaches to quality assurance in education, including both internal and external quality assurance. Internal quality assurance involves self-assessment and self-evaluation, whereas external quality assurance involves an independent evaluation of the educational programs and services. Niu explains that external quality assurance is often conducted by accreditation agencies or governmental bodies and that it provides valuable feedback to organizations about the quality of their educational programs and services.

QUALITY ASSURANCE AND A CADENCE OF ACCOUNTABILITY

We have established quality assurance is a critical aspect of any organization that seeks to maintain high standards and deliver superior results or services to its customers. It is a systematic process that ensures the consistent quality of outcomes and services by identifying and mitigating errors, deviations, and discrepancies throughout the entire production process.[17] A crucial element of implementing an effective quality assurance system is establishing a cadence of accountability, which refers to the regular monitoring and evaluation of performance metrics to ensure that the organization remains aligned with its goals and objectives.[18]

The importance of building a cadence of accountability within the context of quality assurance cannot be overstated. By promoting accountability at all levels of the organization, the likelihood of errors and nonconformances is significantly reduced, leading to improved quality of outcomes.[19] Moreover, the consistent monitoring of performance metrics helps create a culture of continuous improvement, wherein individuals and teams proactively seek opportunities to enhance their performance and contribute to the overall success of the organization. Great school boards know that building a cadence of accountability is a requisite for success.

Each school district is unique; however, to design effective accountability structures, it is essential to focus on inputs as a means of developing accurate reporting mechanisms for progress. Inputs refer to the resources, information, and processes required to produce a desired output. By measuring and evaluating these inputs, organizations can identify areas of inefficiency, waste, or suboptimal performance and implement targeted interventions to drive improvement.[20] A strong board and superintendent leadership team will identify which inputs are likely to have the greatest impact on outcomes and design the cadence of accountability around these inputs in a way that is both meaningful and timely.

By focusing on inputs, we can design accountability structures as accurate reporting mechanisms for progress. Accountability structures that emphasize inputs provide a clear and direct link between individual and team performance and the overall quality of the products or services being delivered. These structures serve as a valuable feedback loop for employees, enabling them to better understand the consequences of their actions and decisions and to identify areas for improvement. This feedback loop, in turn, fosters a sense of ownership and responsibility for the quality of work being produced, which has been shown to enhance employee motivation, satisfaction, and commitment to the organization.[21]

There are several ways to design input-focused accountability structures, and one of the most notable is key performance indicators (KPIs). KPIs are quantifiable metrics that reflect the performance of an individual, team, or organization in relation to specific goals or objectives. By selecting KPIs that are directly related to the inputs that drive quality, organizations can create a performance management system that incentivizes employees to prioritize and focus on the factors that directly contribute to the quality of products or services being delivered.[22]

In addition to KPIs, organizations can further enhance their input-focused accountability structures by embracing continuous improvement methodologies such as Lean and Six Sigma.[23] These methodologies emphasize the identification and elimination of waste and variation within processes, thereby ensuring that inputs are used in the most efficient and effective manner possible. By incorporating these principles into their accountability structures, organizations can further strengthen their focus on inputs and drive ongoing improvements in quality.

The development of a cadence of accountability within the context of quality assurance is of paramount importance for school districts seeking to maintain high standards and deliver exceptional products or services. By focusing on inputs and designing accountability structures that prioritize accurate reporting mechanisms for progress, school districts can create a culture of continuous improvement that drives performance excellence and ultimately leads to enhanced educational outcomes and student success.

A POLICY FOR QUALITY ASSURANCE?

A school board can (and should) write a policy about the importance of having quality assurance frameworks in place before instituting transformative change within the district. Such a policy would outline the importance of having quality assurance frameworks in place to ensure that transformative change is implemented effectively, efficiently, and in a manner that supports the mission and vision of the organization.

The policy should outline the steps that should be taken to develop and implement quality assurance frameworks, including the development of quality standards, training of staff, the collection and analysis of data, and the continuous improvement of educational programs and services. The policy could also outline the importance of involving all stakeholders, including teachers, students, and parents, in the quality assurance process to ensure that their needs and expectations are being met.

Having a policy in place that emphasizes the importance of quality assurance frameworks before instituting transformative change within the district is important for several reasons some of which are self-evident. First, it ensures the changes being made are aligned with the organization's mission and vision (a board prerogative). Second, it provides a systematic approach to ensuring quality and facilitates continuous improvement (a necessary component for positive student outcomes). Third, it ensures that the resources invested in education are used effectively and efficiently (chapter 1). Finally, it ensures that all stakeholders are involved in the quality assurance process and that their needs and expectations are being met (foreshadowing chapter 3).

IMPACT

As with chapter 1, we will pivot to the conclusion by asking what impact does quality assurance frameworks have on the system or community, and how does this relate to the overarching framework of this book? The answers are eerily similar to the first chapter, transparency, trust, enhanced communication, and maintaining a culture of continuous improvement.

It is clear that quality assurance frameworks with a cadence of accountability foster transparency and trust within educational institutions and their larger communities.[24] By regularly reporting on performance metrics, institutions demonstrate their commitment to upholding high standards and being accountable to their stakeholders. This transparency builds trust among the institution, students, parents, and the broader community because they can observe the institution's ongoing efforts to maintain and enhance the quality of education provided.[25]

Incorporating a cadence of accountability within quality assurance frameworks also facilitates better communication among all stakeholders in the educational ecosystem.[26] By providing regular updates on performance metrics, institutions create an open dialogue with their community, allowing for feedback and input from various perspectives. This ongoing communication helps to ensure that the institution's goals and objectives remain relevant and aligned with the needs and expectations of their stakeholders.[27]

Finally, implementing quality assurance frameworks with a cadence of accountability promotes a culture of continuous improvement within educational institutions.[28] By regularly evaluating performance metrics and using the data to inform decision-making, institutions can identify areas for enhancement and develop targeted interventions for improvement. The emphasis on ongoing assessment and improvement fosters a growth mindset among educators and administrators, encouraging them to actively seek opportunities for professional development and innovation.[29]

If we genuinely endeavor to transform the supportive systemic structures that make for great schools (as the framework that is the subject of this book does), then it becomes abundantly clear that quality assurance frameworks and a cadence of accountability are a critical piece of the puzzle. These cannot come first, obviously, because setting quality assurance frameworks for a transformative program cannot happen until there is a program/plan. And as we learned in chapter 1, there can be no program or plan without equitable funding structures. Put differently, equitable funding structures make quality assurance frameworks both necessary and possible.

Further, we have made the case that there are tremendous benefits of implementing internal and external quality assurance frameworks in education. We should not underestimate the importance of involving all stakeholders, including teachers, students, and parents, in the quality assurance process because this serves as a lynchpin into the next chapter. By involving all stakeholders in the quality assurance process, educational organizations can ensure that their programs and services are meeting the needs of all stakeholders and that they are providing a high-quality education to all students. These frameworks provide a systematic approach to ensuring quality and facilitate continuous improvement. By implementing quality assurance frameworks, educational organizations can ensure that their programs and services are aligned with their mission and vision and that they are meeting the desired quality standards.

NOTES

1. Shepherd, *The Secret to Transformational Leadership*.
2. National Commission on Excellence in Education, *A Nation at Risk*.
3. No Child Left Behind Act of 2001, Pub. L. No. 107–110, 115 Stat. 1425.
4. National Center for Education Statistics, *Revenues and Expenditures for Public Elementary and Secondary Education: FY 82–FY19*.
5. Every Student Succeeds Act of 2015, Pub. L. No. 114–95, 129 Stat. 1802.
6. Mullis et al., *TIMSS 2015 International Results in Mathematics*.
7. Tanner, *Community-Based Accountability*.
8. California Department of Education, "California School Dashboard."

9. Oregon Department of Education, "Oregon's Community-Based Accountability System."
10. Shewhart, *Economic Control of Quality of Manufactured Product*.
11. Deming, *Out of the Crisis*.
12. Council for Higher Education Accreditation, "CHEA Recognition Policy and Procedures."
13. Accrediting Commission for Schools, Western Association of Schools and Colleges, "Accreditation Criteria."
14. Baltimore City Public Schools, "Quality Assurance Review (QAR)."
15. National Center for Education Evaluation and Regional Assistance, *Quality Assurance Review of Baltimore City Public Schools: Final Report*.
16. Niu, "Quality Assurance in Education."
17. Oakland, *Total Quality Management and Operational Excellence*.
18. McChesney, Covey, and Huling, *The 4 Disciplines of Execution*.
19. Goetsch and Davis, *Quality Management for Organizational Excellence*.
20. Juran and Godfrey, *Juran's Quality Handbook*, 5th ed.
21. Amabile, "Motivating Creativity in Organizations."
22. Parmenter, *Key Performance Indicators*.
23. George, Rowlands, Price, and Maxey, *The Lean Six Sigma Pocket Toolbook*.
24. Harvey and Newton, "Transforming Quality Evaluation."
25. Middlehurst, "Quality Assurance Implications of New Forms of Higher Education."
26. Jennings and Rentner, "Ten Big Effects of the No Child Left Behind Act on Public Schools."
27. Kettunen, "Implementation of Strategies in Continuing Education and Training."
28. Cheng and Tam, "Multi-Models of Quality in Education."
29. Biesta, *Good Education in an Age of Measurement*.

Chapter 3

Fostering Community-Wide Ownership of Learning

In our rapidly evolving educational landscape, it has become increasingly evident that many of the traditional models of school leadership and administration are no longer sufficient to meet the needs of our students. The time has come for a new paradigm, one that is centered on fostering a culture of ownership around student learning.

Chapters 1 and 2 are critical first steps, as articulated. These first two chapters have slowly been building capacity for chapter 3. Certainly, some readers may read this chapter and think that ownership is where the entire process of building a strong foundation for transformation should start, but this is incorrect. Saying the word *ownership* and actually doing the work of creating ownership are two different things. Many superintendents and board members alike have fallen flat with their community by using the phrase ownership culture without first proving themselves by demonstrating it in action. Note that equitable funding structures are built with full community view and participation. This is community-wide signaling. Building quality assurance frameworks and establishing a cadence of accountability are also ownership building efforts. This chapter will delve into the significance of this approach and outline the essential steps required for successfully building a culture of ownership within a transformational school district.

Throughout this book, we are building a case that leadership in the transformational space is a complex and multifaceted concept that encompasses a wide range of practices and techniques deployed in various contexts to influence, motivate, and guide others . . . and it requires us to think differently about *how* we do the work that we do. Two such concepts that have garnered significant attention in recent years are ownership and engagement. While they may appear similar in some aspects, these concepts exhibit crucial differences in their underlying principles and functional impacts. Throughout this chapter, we will explore the similarities and differences between ownership and engagement, focusing on the assumption of problem-solving in each and their functional consequences.

OWNERSHIP VERSUS BUY-IN OR ENGAGEMENT: A QUICK COMPARATIVE ANALYSIS

Leadership in the transformational space is a complex and multifaceted concept that encompasses a wide range of practices and techniques deployed in various contexts to influence, motivate, and guide others. Two such concepts that have garnered significant attention in recent years are ownership and engagement. While they may appear similar in some aspects, these concepts exhibit crucial differences in their underlying principles and functional impacts. In this section, we will explore the similarities and differences between ownership and engagement, focusing on the assumption of problem-solving in each and their functional consequences.

At first glance, ownership and engagement share several commonalities. Both concepts emphasize the importance of active participation and commitment of all members within an organization or team.[1] This involvement is often achieved by fostering a sense of belonging, motivation, and personal investment in the goals and objectives of the group.[2] Additionally, both ownership and engagement seek to create an environment where individuals feel empowered to take responsibility for their actions and decisions, ultimately promoting a culture of accountability and mutual trust.[3]

Despite these similarities, there are crucial distinctions between ownership and engagement that are particularly evident in the context of problem-solving and leadership dynamics. Engagement, as a leadership concept, presupposes that the leader has a predetermined answer or solution, and their primary objective is to engage followers to support and execute this solution.[4] This approach often involves the leader persuading or motivating followers to align their actions with the leader's vision, fostering a sense of shared purpose and commitment to the established goals.[5] When you hear words like *engagement* or *buy-in*, it is a marker for you that the problem has already been solved and the leader is trying to get others to agree on the solution.

On the other hand, ownership is centered on the premise that leaders and followers work together to authentically solve complex and unknowable problems.[6] This approach necessitates that the leader relinquishes some control and embraces the idea that followers have valuable insights and contributions to offer in the problem-solving process.[7] By fostering a collaborative environment where all members of the team have a voice and are encouraged to take responsibility for their decisions, ownership promotes a greater sense of investment in the outcomes and creates a stronger commitment to the shared objectives.[8]

You may be wondering why this distinction between engagement and ownership matters, and the answer lies in a question, "what does it do?" The functional consequences of ownership and engagement as leadership concepts vary significantly. Engagement, with its focus on persuading followers to align with the leader's predetermined solution, can lead to increased motivation, commitment, and productivity in the short term.[9] However, it may also create a dependence on the leader and stifle creativity and innovation because followers may become overly reliant on the leader's guidance and direction.[10]

In contrast, ownership's emphasis on collaborative problem-solving and shared responsibility can foster a more sustainable and adaptable culture within an organization or team.[11] This is why ownership is a bedrock principle in building a supportive systemic structure that supports transformational leadership. By empowering individuals to take responsibility for their decisions and actions, ownership can promote increased resilience, creativity, and adaptability in the face of complex challenges and changing circumstances.[12] This, in turn, helps the organization reinforce trust, communication, and transparency with all stakeholders.

Although ownership and engagement are two leadership concepts that share similarities in their emphasis on active participation and commitment, they differ significantly in their approach to problem-solving and their functional impacts. Whereas engagement centers on persuading followers to support the leader's predetermined solution, ownership encourages a more collaborative and authentic problem-solving process. The functional consequences of each concept differ, with engagement potentially leading to short-term motivation but stifling innovation, and ownership fostering a more adaptable and innovative organizational culture. For the purposes of building supportive systemic structures for transformation, ownership is the only choice. Given the advantages of ownership in promoting adaptability, creativity, and resilience within organizations, it is worth exploring how to develop a culture of ownership in greater depth.

THE RISE OF OWNERSHIP—A PRIMER

Educational leaders face a myriad of challenges in today's complex and ever-evolving landscape, including the need to improve student outcomes, address equity issues, and adapt to new technologies and instructional approaches. In this context, traditional leadership models may no longer suffice, necessitating the exploration of alternative paradigms that can better equip leaders to navigate these challenges effectively. One such paradigm is *extreme ownership*, a leadership philosophy developed by Willink and Babin[13] in their seminal book, *Extreme Ownership: How U.S. Navy SEALs Lead and Win*. Building on this foundation, Willink and Babin[14] further elaborated on the nuanced nature of leadership in *The Dichotomy of Leadership: Balancing the Challenges of Extreme Ownership to Lead and Win*. Understanding the core principles of extreme ownership and the key leadership factors that make it possible, this section will provide a baseline for educational leaders, which will be applied in the remainder of this chapter as insights and strategies for applying these principles to organizations.

Extreme ownership core principles: At the heart of extreme ownership is the idea that leaders must take full responsibility for the success or failure of their teams and organizations. This mindset is predicated on the following core principles:[15]

1. Take responsibility: Leaders must own the outcomes of their teams and organizations, accepting responsibility for all aspects of their performance, including failures.
2. Prioritize and execute: Leaders must focus on the most critical priorities and ensure that their teams are working toward clear, achievable goals.
3. Decentralize command: Leaders must empower their subordinates to make decisions and take responsibility for their actions, fostering a culture of trust and accountability.
4. Lead up and down the chain of command: Leaders must effectively communicate with both their superiors and subordinates, ensuring that everyone is aligned and working toward common objectives.

The *Dichotomy of Leadership* key factors: In addition to the core principles of extreme ownership, Willink and Babin identify several key leadership factors that must be balanced to successfully implement this philosophy:[16]

1. Balancing confidence and humility: Leaders must exhibit confidence in their abilities while remaining humble enough to learn from their mistakes and seek input from others.
2. Navigating the balance between micromanagement and hands-off leadership: Leaders must strike the right balance between providing guidance and support while granting their subordinates the autonomy to make decisions and take ownership of their actions.
3. Balancing mission accomplishment and troop welfare: Leaders must prioritize achieving organizational goals while also attending to the well-being and development of their team members.
4. In an era of rapid change and increasing demands on educational leaders, the need for effective and adaptive leadership is paramount and our ability to apply this leadership to education could not be more critical.

A CULTURE OF OWNERSHIP IN EDUCATION: THE FOUNDATION OF TRANSFORMATIONAL LEADERSHIP

From *The Secret to Transformational Leadership*, we learn the importance of cultivating a culture of ownership within an educational organization. This critical mindset shift can lead to dramatic improvements in both student achievement and school climate. Ownership, in this context, refers to the extent to which all stakeholders—administrators, teachers, support staff, students, and parents—participate in complex problems and opportunities facing a school district. Complex problems are inherently unknowable, so any approach that values one voice more than others is essentially building the opposite of ownership, which is a culture of buy-in.

A culture of ownership transcends the traditional boundaries of individual classrooms and schools, spreading across the district to create a shared sense of responsibility for the success of the schools, success in student learning, and in actively pursuing its goals. This sense of ownership imbues all stakeholders—students, teachers, administrators, and community members alike—with the power and motivation to work together toward a common goal: the success of every learner.

Creating a culture of ownership is crucial to the architecture of a transformational school district because it fundamentally changes the way schools operate. Instead of fostering a top-down hierarchy, a culture of ownership empowers all stakeholders to take charge of their roles, collaborate, and contribute to the collective success of the organization. By doing so, the focus shifts from mere compliance to a genuine desire for improvement, which ultimately benefits students and the entire school community. So how can we, as transformational leaders, foster such a culture of ownership within our school districts?

KEY FACTORS AND PRACTICES THAT CONTRIBUTE TO BUILDING A CULTURE OF OWNERSHIP

Establish a clear vision and develop shared goals. A well-defined and inspiring vision is the foundation of any transformative endeavor in education. The vision should delineate the desired future state of the school district, emphasizing the core values that will steer the journey. By fostering a shared sense of purpose, the vision acts as a guiding light, uniting stakeholders and encouraging ownership of student learning. Building a strong culture of ownership starts with a clear, persuasive vision of the school district's objectives. This vision must be in tune with the needs of the students and the community, serving as a reference point for all decision-making processes. Involving all stakeholders in crafting this vision and setting shared goals is crucial, as it cultivates a feeling of collective ownership from the beginning.

Nearly every school district has a vision, mission, and goals, which might have been established recently or inherited from past generations. Both situations are valid. It is important to note that this text is not focused on creating an ideal school district from scratch; instead, it aims to take a school district, regardless of its current state, and guide it toward improvement. Hence, we did not begin with a discussion about vision and mission. The existing vision and mission statements most likely mention concepts such as "all children, continuous improvement, excellence, and outcomes" or similar themes.

These principles are sufficient to commence the process of creating equitable funding structures. Only after undertaking this work, as well as implementing quality assurance measures, can we reevaluate the vision for transformation, allowing for a more profound and impactful change in the educational landscape.

BUILD QUALITY ASSURANCE FRAMEWORKS

As discussed in great depth in chapter 2, building quality assurance frameworks is a necessary component to building an ownership culture. By embracing an ownership mindset, leaders can model and encourage a culture of responsibility, where people own their actions and their impact on student outcomes. This shift in mindset can lead to increased collaboration, a stronger commitment to continuous improvement, and ultimately, better results for students.

EMPOWER TEACHERS AND STAFF

One of the most effective ways to cultivate a culture of ownership is by empowering teachers and students to take charge of their own learning. By decentralizing command and empowering teachers and staff to make decisions and take responsibility for their actions, educational leaders can foster a sense of ownership and investment in the success of the organization. This empowerment can result in increased motivation, creativity, and innovation, ultimately benefiting student outcomes.

By providing the necessary support and resources, transformational leaders enable teachers to personalize instruction and employ innovative teaching practices. Concurrently, students are encouraged to take responsibility for their learning journey, set goals, and collaborate with peers and teachers to achieve them. In this environment, both teachers and students are vested in each other's growth and success.

Collaboration is a powerful force for change. When schools work together, sharing best practices and resources, the impact on student learning is magnified. Transformational leaders create opportunities for collaboration within and between schools, establishing networks and platforms for knowledge exchange. By connecting teachers, administrators, and students in this way, they pave the way for collective ownership of student learning.

To build a culture of ownership, it is vital to empower teachers and staff by giving them the autonomy, resources, and support they need to excel in their roles. Encourage professional development and provide opportunities for collaboration, allowing educators to learn from one another and grow together. Recognize and celebrate their successes and treat setbacks as opportunities for growth and improvement.

ENCOURAGE STUDENT VOICE AND AGENCY

Students hold a central role in the educational process, and fostering their active involvement in learning is essential for cultivating a sense of ownership. To encourage student voice and agency, educators must create opportunities for students to express their opinions, contribute to decision-making processes, and assume responsibility for their learning outcomes. By promoting a growth mindset and building resilience, educators can empower students to recognize their capacity to overcome obstacles and achieve success.

To establish a true culture of ownership in education, it is vital to involve students in addressing organizational challenges and learning impediments that have persisted for years. Often, those most intimately affected by these issues possess valuable insight into potential solutions. Put differently, those closest to the problem should have the greatest voice in solving that problem. By granting students the opportunity to contribute meaningfully to problem-solving, an ownership mindset is more likely to flourish. In the majority of instances, the most effective resolutions will emerge when all voices are considered and valued equally.

Building an ownership culture necessitates the inclusion of everyone within the educational community and not just a select few. This means involving all students, not just a select few to represent the student body, in these collaborative efforts to drive improvement. Schools can implement strategies such as student-led conferences, peer-mentoring programs, and collaborative project-based learning to facilitate this sense of ownership. Additionally, incorporating student feedback into curriculum and policy decisions reinforces the message that their voices matter.

Ultimately, promoting a culture of ownership in education hinges on acknowledging the critical role students play in shaping their learning experiences. By empowering them to take an active role in decision-making and problem-solving, educators can create an environment where students thrive and become resilient, lifelong learners.

PARENTS AND THE COMMUNITY

Parents and the community play a significant role in shaping a culture of ownership. Parents and community members are active partners in the educational process, and we must create opportunities for meaningful collaboration, communication, and involvement. Seek both their feedback and feed-forward. Feedback tells you who you are. Feed-forward tells you who you are *becoming*. Feedback is a form of accountability, and feed-forward is a form of input. At the deepest levels of ownership, we ask for more feed-forward than feedback. By doing so, you will create a strong network of support and shared responsibility for the success of the school district.

The community is an invaluable resource in the quest for transformational change. By involving families, businesses, and local organizations in the educational process, leaders can tap into a vast reservoir of support and expertise. There are myriad ways to bring parents and community closer to our schools to build an ownership culture around decision-making and what follows is not an exhaustive list. However, here are a few examples for consideration:

1. Create a community task force around nearly any complex issue: Education leaders can host community taskforce (or committee, or roundtable, what you call it does not matter) discussions to bring parents, community members, and business leaders together to share their perspectives, ideas, and concerns. This can help to create a sense of shared responsibility and ownership among all stakeholders.
2. Host a business luncheon: Education leaders can invite local business leaders to a luncheon at the school to discuss how the school and the business community can work together to improve the school's performance. This can also help to build partnerships and increase the school's visibility in the community. Many school districts already do this. Some are formal, and some are highly informal.
3. Organize a realtor open house: Education leaders can invite real estate agents to visit the school to see firsthand what the school has to offer. This can help to promote the school throughout the community.
4. Develop a culture of empowerment: Education leaders can foster a culture of empowerment by modeling responsible behavior, communicating the organization's values and goals, providing opportunities for professional development, and establishing clear guidelines and expectations for behavior. This can create a culture that values collaboration, creativity, and innovation, and fosters a sense of ownership among all members.
5. Encourage parent and community involvement: Education leaders can encourage parents and community members to get involved in school activities, such as volunteering, attending school events, and participating in school decision-making processes. This can help to create a sense of ownership and investment in the school's success. Savvy education leaders also realize the importance of building a leadership ladder that

exists outside the school walls. They recognize a PTO president may be a good fit for a leadership role in a task force, for instance.
6. Provide training for parent and community leaders: Education leaders can ensure we provide training and support for parent and community leaders to help them develop the skills and knowledge they need to effectively contribute to school improvement efforts.
7. Use social media: Education leaders can use social media platforms to promote the school's achievements, share information about upcoming events, and solicit feedback from parents and community members. This can help to increase engagement and involvement in the school.

Through partnerships, internships, and community service projects, students gain real-world experience and insights that enrich their learning. In turn, the community becomes invested in the success of the school district, contributing to a culture of ownership.

NAVIGATING OWNERSHIP—SPECIAL CONSIDERATIONS FOR LEADERS

Educational leaders can benefit from understanding and navigating the key leadership factors discussed, and by striking the right balance between these factors, leaders can create a more effective and adaptive leadership style.

We must balance confidence and humility. Educational leaders must be confident in their knowledge and abilities while remaining humble enough to learn from their mistakes, seek input from others, and recognize the expertise and contributions of their team members. This balance can lead to increased trust and collaboration, resulting in a more supportive and effective learning environment for students.

Only with a balance of confidence and humility can a leader understand and make use of the difference among making space, holding space, and filling space. All too often, leaders do all three. A deeply held ownership culture will find the leader making space (sometimes), holding space (often), and filling space (rarely). Making space is simply the act of bringing people together. The question becomes what people and what does together mean? Leaders are overt and conscientious about how and where they make space for dialogue. Holding space is all about safety and security. The space must be a place where all voices participate equally. The space must be a safe place for all thoughts and viewpoints to be shared. Only with a sense of group safety will open and honest dialogue take place. Filling space are the things we do in that space. If they include slide presentations, speeches, staged responses, or the like, the leader is filling space and this is antithetical to an ownership culture.

Education leaders must navigate the balance between micromanagement and hands-off leadership. Leaders must find the right balance between providing guidance and support to their teams while allowing them the autonomy to make decisions and take ownership of their actions. By striking this balance, leaders can foster a sense of empowerment and ownership among their teams, leading to increased innovation, creativity, and student success. Often, if the leader is too close to the action, the pace will slow. Leaders bring a sense of gravity (mass) with them in a very real sense. We know from physics that mass exerts an interesting force on time. More mass means time slows down. This principle from physics applies directly to leadership. This very thing has likely happened to you in the past, and there is a high likelihood you have also caused it to happen. This must be balanced with being too far from the problem or solution and losing a sense of the work being done. Mastering the art of distance is key.

Finally, leaders must balance mission and welfare. Educational leaders must prioritize achieving organizational goals while also attending to the well-being and development of their team members. By balancing these competing priorities, leaders can create a more sustainable and effective educational organization that is better equipped to support student success.

Educational organizations can create an environment where all members feel empowered to take responsibility for their decisions and actions by implementing effective leadership actions and fostering a culture of empowerment. Leaders must model responsible behavior, communicate the organization's values and goals, provide opportunities for professional development, and establish clear guidelines and expectations for behavior. By doing so, they can create a culture that values collaboration, creativity, and innovation and fosters a sense of ownership among all members.

A POLICY FOR OWNERSHIP?

Creating an ownership culture in education means empowering stakeholders to take an active role in decision-making. As described throughout this chapter, this can be achieved through promoting open communication, encouraging collaboration, and providing opportunities for feedback and reflection. When stakeholders feel ownership, they are more invested in the outcomes and are more likely to take responsibility for the success or failure of decisions. As such, it is important to consider whether a policy requiring ownership for collaborative decision-making is necessary. While such a policy may help to formalize and institutionalize the culture of ownership, it is also important to ensure the policy is practical, effective, and aligned with the values and goals of the organization. Ultimately, the decision to write a policy requiring ownership for collaborative decision-making should be made with careful consideration of the specific context and needs of the organization. What follows is a nonexhaustive list of arguments in favor and against such a policy.

Arguments in favor of creating a policy about collaborative decision-making for all decisions:

1. Increases unity: When people are involved in the decision-making process, they are more likely to feel ownership of the outcome. By involving stakeholders in decisions, you can increase the level unity in commitment to the decision, which can lead to better implementation and outcomes.
2. Encourages participation: Collaborative decision-making encourages participation from all members of the group, which can lead to a more diverse set of perspectives and ideas. This can result in better decision-making as well as increased engagement and satisfaction from participants.
3. Builds trust: Collaborative decision-making can help to build trust between members of the group. By involving all stakeholders in the process, everyone can see that their input is valued and that decisions are being made in a fair and transparent manner.

Arguments against creating a policy about collaborative decision-making for all decisions:

1. Can be time-consuming: Collaborative decision-making can be a time-consuming process. In some cases, it may be more efficient for a small group of individuals to make a decision rather than involving everyone in the process.
2. Can be difficult to manage: Collaborative decision-making can be difficult to manage, especially if there are conflicting opinions or personalities within the group. Polarities within, among, and between group members may develop and grow if not managed correctly. This can lead to delays or disagreements that can impede progress.
3. May not be appropriate for all decisions: Collaborative decision-making may not be appropriate for all decisions. For example, decisions that require a high degree of expertise or technical knowledge (complicated decisions where there is just one right answer) may be better made by a smaller group of experts rather than involving everyone in the process.

Overall, while collaborative decision-making can have many benefits, it may not be appropriate for all decisions. The board of education should consider the potential benefits and drawbacks of such a policy and determine whether it is appropriate for their organization. They should also consider ways to manage the process effectively, such as establishing clear roles and responsibilities and providing training or resources to support collaborative decision-making.

This answer may seem insufficient to many of you reading this book. If so, this is wonderful news as the next two chapters will address this concept in greater detail. We may not get closer to one right answer, but you will feel much more confident in your approach.

IMPACT

Fostering ownership of student learning within the community is a critical aspect in building the supportive systemic structures that allow for transformation in our schools to take place on a firm foundation of stone. As discussed throughout this chapter, it takes the involvement of various stakeholders, including parents, teachers, staff, and students, to create an ownership culture. As with previous chapters, we will now examine the impact of fostering ownership of student learning within the community. At this point, you may note five essential themes continue to resurface: transparency, trust, enhanced communication, better decision-making, and maintaining a culture of improvement.

Ownership creates better transparency in education through the open and honest sharing of information. Radical transparency is simply having discipline to create unprecedented levels of access to both people and to information. Research has shown that transparency is positively associated with improved student outcomes.[17] Furthermore, transparency in education leads to more informed decision-making, improved student outcomes, and a culture of continuous improvement.[18] Some might think transparency is enough, but applying transparency to the concept of ownership creates a two-way street. The district must be engaged in a regular dialogue with the community. This means sometimes sharing information and sometimes asking questions.

Trust is a critical component of any successful educational community. As education leaders our currency is trust. Fostering ownership of student learning within the community is a self-reinforcing concept of building trust between and among stakeholders. Teachers, staff, and administrators must earn the trust of parents and the community by creating an environment of transparency, open communication, and accountability. Research has shown that trust is positively associated with improved student outcomes.[19] Furthermore, trust enables stakeholders to work together to create a shared vision for educational success and fosters a sense of ownership and commitment to student learning.[20]

Effective communication is essential in fostering ownership of student learning within the community. As previously discussed, communication is a two-way process that should involve equal parts listening to the needs of stakeholders and sharing information about student progress, school policies, and procedures. Research has shown that effective communication is positively associated with improved student outcomes.[21] Furthermore, effective communication enables parents, teachers, staff, and students to collaborate and share ideas, leading to better decision-making and improved student outcomes.[22]

Fostering ownership of student learning within the community requires a culture of continuous improvement. This culture requires stakeholders to work together to identify areas for improvement and collaborate to implement meaningful changes. It involves a commitment to ongoing professional development, data analysis, and collaboration. When stakeholders are committed to continuous improvement, they create a culture of ownership and accountability, resulting in improved student outcomes.[23]

Fostering ownership of student learning within the community requires a collaborative approach to decision-making. When stakeholders have access to school data and effective communication channels, they can collaborate to identify areas for improvement and make data-driven decisions. This approach leads to better decision-making and results in improved student outcomes. Furthermore, involving stakeholders in the decision-making process creates a sense of ownership and commitment to student learning.[24]

A FINAL NOTE ABOUT COLLABORATION AND OWNERSHIP

In the realm of education, numerous school districts grapple with the challenge of fostering true ownership in collaborative decision-making. While they may claim to embrace collaboration, it is not uncommon for decisions to be partially or entirely predetermined before involving the community. This approach has contributed to a growing disconnect between the public and public education. To reestablish the relationship between the two, it is crucial that educational institutions refrain from presenting the community with predetermined solutions to complex, multifaceted problems. This is how we bring the public back to public education.

Examples of such issues include determining the timing and amount of a bond campaign, rezoning decisions, tax rate adjustments, school closures or openings, mergers, and decisions related to budget deficits and program cuts. None of these dilemmas have a single, definitive solution. When a district assembles a group of "smart people" (however defined) to devise a plan without involving the full community, it undermines the essence of ownership and the spirit of collaboration.

To cultivate a sense of ownership around these complex problems, educational leaders must adopt a compassionate, transparent, and inclusive approach. This entails openly communicating the challenges faced by the district, informing the community of the intentions to address these issues, and actively soliciting their involvement in finding solutions. It is essential to create opportunities for all interested parties to participate, ensuring that each voice is heard and respected, regardless of background or expertise. Anything less than this level of inclusivity detracts from the goal of genuine ownership.

Adopting this vulnerable and, at times, intimidating leadership style can be daunting. However, it is the only way to foster true ownership and effectively engage the community in the decision-making process. By doing so, educational institutions can bridge the divide between the public and public education, leading to more resilient and effective solutions that reflect the diverse perspectives and needs of the community.

NOTES

1. Covey, *The 7 Habits of Highly Effective People*.
2. Wagner and Harter, *12: The Elements of Great Managing*.
3. Sinek, *Leaders Eat Last*.
4. Pink, *Drive*.
5. Kotter, *Leading Change*.
6. Heifetz and Linsky, *Leadership on the Line*.
7. Collins, *Good to Great*.
8. Heifetz, Grashow, and Linsky, *The Practice of Adaptive Leadership*.
9. Pink, *Drive*.
10. Heifetz and Linsky, *Leadership on the Line*.
11. Heifetz, Grashow, and Linsky, *The Practice of Adaptive Leadership*.
12. Collins, *Good to Great*.
13. Willink and Babin, *Extreme Ownership*.
14. Willink and Babin, *The Dichotomy of Leadership*.
15. Willink and Babin, *Extreme Ownership*.
16. Willink and Babin, *The Dichotomy of Leadership*.
17. Headden, "Why School Transparency Is Important."
18. McDonnell, Socolar, and Kirschner, *A Path Forward*.
19. Bryk and Schneider, "Trust in Schools."

20. Bryk, Sebring, Allensworth, Luppescu, and Easton, *Organizing Schools for Improvement*.

21. Bryk, Sebring, Allensworth, Luppescu, and Easton, *Organizing Schools for Improvement*.

22. Epstein, Sanders, Simon, Salinas, Jansorn, and Van Voorhis, *School, Family, and Community Partnerships*.

23. Bryk, Sebring, Allensworth, Luppescu, and Easton, *Organizing Schools for Improvement*.

24. Bryk, Sebring, Allensworth, Luppescu, and Easton, *Organizing Schools for Improvement*.

Chapter 4

Courageous Leadership and Policymaking

As we delve into this chapter, you may initially believe that the presented framework is out of sequence. It is a common belief that courageous leadership is a prerequisite for any grand, transformative action or change. You might even assume that it requires courage to address the issues at hand. However, this mindset may not actually facilitate problem-solving. Although this form of courage might propel you into a challenge, it may not guarantee your emergence from it. Consider the analogy of leaping into a freezing lake; taking the plunge requires courage, but the real challenge lies in enduring the icy waters and going for a swim. This example illustrates a vital point about leadership courage: Many leaders can muster the bravery to take the leap, but far fewer possess the fortitude to persevere. While initial acts of courage may garner praise, it is long-term, disciplined courage that truly inspires and encourages others to be courageous as well.

In this chapter, we will explore the courage not only to confront problems or embark on transformational endeavors but also the resilience to see these initiatives through and make meaningful progress. Throughout the chapter, you will gain insights into the significance of this courageous leadership, how it can be defined, its sources of power, and why it is indispensable for transformational change. Furthermore, we will examine the relationship between courageous leadership and policymaking, highlighting the importance of creating and implementing policies that encourage innovation and support educational reform. By understanding the intricacies of courageous leadership and the impact of supportive policies, you will be better equipped to foster a culture of courage and resilience in your educational environment, ultimately paving the way for meaningful, lasting change.

COURAGEOUS LEADERSHIP: A NECESSARY ATTRIBUTE FOR EFFECTIVE CHANGE MANAGEMENT

Because the framework for this book starts with creating equitable funding structures and then moves into establishing quality assurance frameworks, the leader has naturally stepped into courageous leadership. It takes great courage to address inequity in funding. It takes great courage to commit to a cadence of accountability as part of a quality assurance framework. Courageous leadership then has been an immersive learning experience up to this point. It has also been discreetly focused on a project or initiative. Because the focus of this book is building a systemic structure that supports transformative change, it is paramount to build courageous leadership into that structure. Continuous improvement for any education institution requires change, and change is hard.

Change management is an essential aspect of an educational organization's success in today's rapidly evolving world. The pace of change continues to increase, and there is no indication the pace of change will slow down. If anything, change will come even faster. The capacity to adapt to change is not only vital for survival but also for thriving in the face of uncertainty. At the heart of effective change management lies courageous leadership. We will explore why courageous leadership is a critical attribute for change management, focusing on the courage required to make changes, institute new ideas, shift personnel, and handle criticism. We will then examine the role of courageous leadership in long-term change management theory and its significance in sustaining initial efforts over time.

NEW INITIATIVES REQUIRE COURAGE

In the field of education, making changes and introducing new ideas demand courage from those in leadership positions. Courageous leadership entails the readiness to question conventional practices and embrace uncertainty.[1] This necessitates leaders to take well-thought-out risks, make difficult decisions, and assume accountability for the results. The courage exhibited by such leaders paves the way for transformative growth, cultivating an environment that nurtures innovation and ongoing enhancement.[2]

For example, a courageous educational leader may advocate for a shift from traditional teaching methods to more student-centered, active learning approaches, even in the face of opposition from faculty who are resistant to change. This leader recognizes the long-term benefits of active learning for student engagement and success and boldly leads the way in implementing these new methodologies.

Another example of courageous leadership in education is the integration of technology in the classroom. Embracing new technologies, such as virtual reality or artificial intelligence, can significantly enhance the learning experience. However, it may also be met with skepticism and resistance from stakeholders who are concerned about the potential loss of personal connections or are hesitant to invest in the required resources. A courageous leader is not deterred by these challenges and actively seeks ways to overcome obstacles, demonstrating the positive impact of these innovations and securing necessary support.

Additionally, courageous leadership in education may involve championing diversity and inclusion initiatives. Despite potential pushback, these leaders recognize the importance of creating an inclusive learning environment that celebrates differences and fosters belonging among students and staff.

This may involve implementing changes in curricula, hiring practices, and institutional policies to ensure equity and representation.

In summary, a courageous leader in the education sector is unafraid to introduce new ideas or refine existing ones, regardless of resistance from stakeholders. By exhibiting unwavering determination and commitment to transformative change, these leaders play a crucial role in shaping the future of education and driving progress in the field.

COURAGE TO SHIFT PERSONNEL AND TAKE CRITICISM

Effective change management demands the courage to undertake essential personnel adjustments. Educational leaders must be willing to make challenging decisions concerning hiring, firing, and reorganizing teams—even when these choices may be met with disapproval.[3] For instance, a principal might have to replace a long-serving but underperforming teacher with a new, innovative educator to improve student outcomes. Similarly, school administrators may have to restructure teams to better allocate resources, such as creating interdisciplinary project teams to address specific school needs.

Courageous leaders in education also appreciate the value of constructive criticism and use it as a chance for growth and learning.[4] They actively seek feedback from various stakeholders, including teachers, students, parents, and support staff, to identify areas of improvement. For example, a school district superintendent might hold town hall meetings, conduct surveys, or establish advisory committees to gather input and insights from the community.

This receptiveness to feedback enables educational leaders to modify their strategies and approaches as necessary, ensuring that they remain in line with the institution's goals and objectives. A department head, for instance, may receive feedback from teachers about the need for additional professional development opportunities in a specific area. As a result, the department head can then allocate resources and develop targeted training programs to address this need, ultimately benefiting both teachers and students.

In short, courageous educational leaders recognize the importance of making tough personnel decisions and embracing constructive criticism as a means of fostering growth and development. Their openness to feedback and adaptability to change ensure that they effectively guide their institutions toward achieving their goals and objectives, ultimately contributing to the betterment of the educational landscape.

LONG-TERM CHANGE MANAGEMENT THEORY AND COURAGEOUS LEADERSHIP

Over the long term, successful change management in the field of education necessitates a continuous commitment from leaders. This unwavering dedication, in turn, calls for courageous leadership to maintain momentum, even when confronted with obstacles or setbacks. Courageous leaders demonstrate resilience in their endeavors, creating an atmosphere that promotes ongoing adaptation and enhancement within the educational institution.[5]

For example, a school district superintendent who initiates a multiyear program and plans to improve student performance may face resistance from some faculty members or budget constraints. Despite these challenges, the courageous leader remains steadfast in their pursuit of improvement, continually seeking innovative solutions and resources to achieve their goals.

Moreover, courageous educational leaders possess the ability to balance competing priorities and interests, ensuring that the organization stays focused on its long-term objectives.[6] In the context of education, this might involve juggling the demands of various stakeholders, such as teachers, students, parents, and regulatory bodies. A school principal, for instance, may have to navigate between the need for standardized test preparation and the desire to incorporate more project-based learning activities, both of which contribute to the school's overall mission of fostering student success.

Long-term change management in education relies on the sustained commitment of courageous leaders who can maintain momentum and persevere through challenges. By fostering an environment that encourages continuous adaptation and improvement and adeptly balancing competing priorities, these leaders effectively guide their organizations toward achieving their long-term goals.

Courageous leadership is a vital attribute for effective change management. Leaders who exhibit courage are better equipped to implement changes, introduce new ideas, make necessary personnel adjustments, and accept criticism. Moreover, courageous leadership is essential for sustaining initial efforts in long-term change management, ensuring that organizations can adapt and thrive in an ever-changing world.

NAVIGATING THE IMPLEMENTATION DIP: THE ROLE OF COURAGEOUS LEADERSHIP

The case has been made that change management is a critical aspect of organizational success, particularly in today's rapidly evolving environment.

Michael Fullan, a renowned educational researcher and change management expert, introduced the concept of the "implementation dip" as a natural part of the change process.[7] The implementation dip refers to the temporary decline in performance that often occurs when new practices or policies are introduced, as individuals adapt to the changes and develop new skills. This section examines the necessity of strong and courageous leadership to navigate the implementation dip effectively, focusing on controlling its depth and duration by addressing the needs of the organization and its members and confronting the facts when things are not going well.

The implementation dip can be a challenging phase in the change process because it can lead to frustration, resistance, and even the abandonment of the new practices or policies.[8] Strong and courageous leadership is essential to guide organizations through the implementation dip, ensuring that the organization remains committed to the change and overcomes any obstacles encountered. Courageous leaders possess the resilience and determination to persevere through the difficulties associated with the implementation dip, providing support and guidance to their team members as they adapt to the changes.[9]

For example, a high school principal decides to implement a flipped classroom model across the school to promote active learning and improve student engagement. The flipped classroom model involves students watching instructional videos or engaging with learning materials at home, while class time is dedicated to discussions, problem-solving, and collaborative activities. During the implementation of this new teaching model, teachers and students may experience an implementation dip.[10] Teachers could struggle to adapt their lesson plans and teaching methods, while students may initially find it challenging to adjust to the new expectations and learning environment. This period of uncertainty and adaptation can lead to frustration, resistance, and potentially even abandonment of the new practices.

To minimize the negative impact of the implementation dip, courageous leaders must focus on controlling its depth and duration. This requires a keen understanding of the needs of the organization and the individuals within it, as well as the willingness to confront the facts when things are not going well.[11] Leaders must actively engage in ongoing communication, providing clear expectations and offering resources and support to help their team members develop the necessary skills and competencies to adapt to the changes.[12]

In the example about a flipped classroom initiative, the principal could:

1. Communicate the rationale and benefits of the flipped classroom model to all stakeholders, including teachers, students, and parents. This can foster understanding and buy-in from the school community, ensuring continued commitment to the change.

2. Provide professional development opportunities for teachers to help them adapt their lesson plans and teaching strategies for the flipped classroom model. This may include workshops, coaching sessions, and opportunities for teachers to observe and learn from colleagues who have successfully implemented the model.
3. Offer ongoing support and resources for teachers during the implementation process, such as access to instructional videos, lesson planning tools, and opportunities for collaboration and peer feedback.
4. Regularly gather feedback from teachers, students, and parents to assess the effectiveness of the flipped classroom model and identify any areas that need improvement. This can help the principal make data-informed decisions to adjust the implementation plan as needed.
5. Celebrate and share successes to maintain morale and momentum throughout the implementation process. Recognizing the achievements of teachers and students who have adapted well to the flipped classroom model can inspire others and reinforce the benefits of the change.

By displaying courageous leadership, the principal can guide the school through the implementation dip, ensuring that the organization remains committed to the change and overcomes any obstacles encountered. Ultimately, the successful implementation of the flipped classroom model can lead to improved student engagement and learning outcomes.

Navigating the implementation dip is an integral aspect of change management, and courageous leadership is essential to guide organizations through this challenging phase. A leader must first embrace that the implementation dip will likely occur. Then, by focusing on the needs of the organization and its members, as well as confronting the facts when things are not going well, courageous leaders can effectively control the depth and length of the implementation dip, ultimately ensuring the successful implementation of change.

COURAGEOUS LEADERSHIP DEFINED

Courageous leadership in an educational context can be defined as the ability of a leader to influence, inspire, and empower others to work together in pursuit of common goals, despite potential risks, challenges, or resistance. This type of leadership is crucial in educational settings because it enables positive change, innovation, and growth for both students and staff. Rost's[13] definition of leadership emphasizes relational, ethical, and goal-oriented aspects of the leader-follower relationship. Based on Rost's definition, courageous leadership in an educational context can be broken down into several key elements:

1. Relational aspect: Courageous leaders foster strong relationships with students, staff, and the wider community. They create an environment that encourages open communication, collaboration, and teamwork. For example, a principal who actively listens to the concerns of teachers and parents and works with them to address these issues demonstrates courageous leadership.
2. Ethical aspect: Courageous leaders uphold and promote ethical values in their educational settings. They lead by example, demonstrating honesty, integrity, and respect for others. An example would be a teacher who addresses instances of bullying in the classroom and promotes a culture of empathy and understanding.
3. Goal-oriented aspect: Courageous leaders are focused on achieving shared goals and are willing to take calculated risks to do so. They push their teams to challenge the status quo, innovate, and strive for continuous improvement. For instance, a school administrator who supports and implements a new curriculum or teaching approach, despite initial resistance from staff, demonstrates courageous leadership.

Insights and examples of courageous leadership in an educational context:

1. A school principal who fights for increased funding and resources for their underprivileged school, risking their reputation or job security to provide better opportunities for students.
2. A teacher who adopts an innovative teaching method, such as project-based learning or flipped classrooms, to better engage students and improve learning outcomes, even if it requires extra effort and initial resistance from students or colleagues.
3. An administrator who advocates for the inclusion of students with special needs, ensuring they receive appropriate support and accommodations in mainstream classrooms, despite potential backlash or logistical challenges.
4. A school counselor who stands up against institutional policies that unfairly disadvantage certain student populations, working to create a more equitable and inclusive environment.
5. A school board member who readily commits to attending community forums to ensure an educational presence is felt throughout the community.

COMPASSIONATE LEADERSHIP IS A PILLAR OF COURAGEOUS LEADERSHIP

The Secret to Transformational Leadership[14] advocates for the value of compassionate leadership as an indispensable component of courageous leadership in education. In it, Shepherd highlights that compassionate leadership as the ability to "suffer with" others, rather than "suffer for" them, emphasizing the importance of empathy, shared experiences, and understanding in fostering a supportive and inclusive educational environment. This section will explore how compassionate leadership makes courageous leadership possible in education and will discuss the various ways this approach benefits both educators and students alike.

According to Shepherd, compassionate leadership is founded on the concept of "compassion" derived from the Latin word *passion*, which means "to suffer." Compassion then is to suffer with. This definition is critical in differentiating compassionate leadership from other forms of empathy-based leadership. When leaders choose to suffer with their colleagues and students, they foster a sense of shared experiences, deep understanding, and mutual support that transcends the traditional hierarchies often present in educational settings.

Compassionate leadership is vital for courageous leadership because it enables educational leaders to navigate the complexities and challenges of their roles with greater resilience, creativity, and conviction. Shepherd argues that the ability to deeply understand and empathize with the struggles and triumphs of others fosters an environment where leaders can take calculated risks, engage in open communication, and address systemic issues that impact the educational community.

Moreover, compassionate leadership serves as a catalyst for courageous leadership by promoting a culture of trust and psychological safety. According to Brené Brown, psychological safety is a critical component of effective and courageous leadership. When leaders demonstrate compassion and empathy, they create an environment where individuals feel comfortable expressing their thoughts, concerns, and ideas without fear of judgment or retribution. This climate of trust and openness empowers educators and students to take risks, learn from mistakes, and engage in collaborative problem-solving.[15]

Additionally, compassionate leadership fosters equity and inclusivity in educational settings. As Sonia Nieto[16] points out, acknowledging and addressing the diverse needs of students and educators is essential for fostering equitable educational environments. Compassionate leaders recognize and validate the unique experiences and perspectives of each individual within their community, creating a space where everyone can thrive.[17]

Being disciplined about compassionate leadership in education offers numerous benefits for both educators and students. Studies have shown that when educational leaders prioritize empathy, collaboration, and shared experiences, they create environments where educators feel valued and supported.[18] This sense of belonging can positively impact job satisfaction, retention rates, and overall performance.

For students, compassionate leadership contributes to a sense of belonging and well-being that is essential for academic success. According to Deci and Ryan's[19] self-determination theory, students are more likely to be engaged and motivated in their learning when they feel connected, supported, and understood by their educators. Compassionate leaders facilitate these connections by promoting empathy, understanding, and inclusivity in their educational communities.[20]

Compassionate leadership as "suffering with" others rather than "suffering for" them is a necessary component of courageous leadership in education because it creates common purpose. This common purpose is what drives the final two pieces of the framework of this book. By fostering empathy, shared experiences, and understanding, compassionate leadership creates environments where trust, psychological safety, and inclusivity can thrive. This approach benefits both educators and students, contributing to a sense of belonging, well-being, and increased academic success. Make no mistake, it takes great courage to lead with compassion because vulnerability stands at the forefront of this style of leadership. By embracing compassionate leadership, educational leaders can navigate the complex challenges of their roles with resilience, creativity, and conviction, ultimately transforming the educational landscape for the better.

UNEARTHING THE SOURCES OF LEADERSHIP COURAGE

Leadership courage is an essential quality for educational leaders as they navigate the complex landscape of contemporary education. Courageous leaders are well-equipped to address the myriad challenges they face, including addressing systemic inequities, fostering inclusive environments, and promoting innovation. This section will explore the sources of leadership courage in the context of education leadership, drawing on three seminal works in the field: Brené Brown's *Dare to Lead*, Parker J. Palmer's *The Courage to Teach*, and Heifetz, Grashow, and Linsky's *The Practice of Adaptive Leadership*. These resources offer unique insights into the origins of courage and the ways in which it can be cultivated by educational leaders.

Vulnerability is a source of courage. Brown's *Dare to Lead* posits that vulnerability is a critical source of courage for educational leaders. Brown argues that embracing vulnerability involves acknowledging one's limitations, being open to feedback, and engaging in difficult conversations. By embracing vulnerability, leaders can cultivate the courage to take risks, make difficult decisions, and address systemic issues within their educational communities.

For educational leaders, vulnerability involves acknowledging the uncertainty and complexity inherent in their work, as well as being open to learning from mistakes and failures. According to Brown, this willingness to embrace vulnerability allows leaders to model humility and resilience, fostering a culture of trust and psychological safety in their educational communities.

Authenticity and self-awareness are a source of courage. In *The Courage to Teach*, Palmer[21] emphasizes the importance of authenticity and self-awareness as sources of courage in educational leadership. Palmer argues that leaders who are deeply connected to their own values, beliefs, and passions can draw on these internal resources to navigate the challenges they face. Authenticity and self-awareness enable leaders to remain grounded in their purpose and convictions, even in the face of adversity and criticism.

For educational leaders, cultivating authenticity and self-awareness involves ongoing reflection, introspection, and a commitment to personal growth. By understanding their own strengths and limitations, as well as their unique motivations and values, leaders can tap into an inner wellspring of courage that enables them to lead with conviction and integrity.

Adaptive leadership is a source of courage. Heifetz, Grashow, and Linsky's *The Practice of Adaptive Leadership*[22] offers a unique perspective on the sources of courage in education leadership by emphasizing the importance of adaptive leadership. Adaptive leadership involves the ability to identify, address, and navigate complex, systemic issues by promoting innovation, collaboration, and learning within an organization.

According to Heifetz, Grashow, and Linsky, cultivating the courage to lead adaptively involves embracing the discomfort and uncertainty that often accompany change. By developing the capacity to identify and address the underlying causes of systemic issues, rather than merely addressing their symptoms, adaptive leaders can cultivate the courage to confront deeply rooted problems and promote meaningful change within their educational communities.

Some sources of leadership courage in the context of education leadership can be found in vulnerability, authenticity, self-awareness, and adaptive leadership. By embracing vulnerability, cultivating authenticity and self-awareness, and developing the capacity for adaptive leadership, educational leaders can draw on these sources of courage to navigate the complex challenges they face. As these seminal works by Brown, Palmer, and Heifetz,

Grashow, and Linsky demonstrate, understanding and cultivating the sources of leadership courage is essential for educational leaders seeking to make a lasting impact on their organizations and the communities they serve.

FOSTERING COLLECTIVE COURAGE FOR TRANSFORMATION: THE ROLE OF THE INDIVIDUAL

Individual courageous leadership is essential for driving transformational change in education at a community scale. This type of leadership enables educational leaders to address systemic issues, foster inclusivity, and promote innovation, ultimately contributing to a more equitable and just educational landscape. This section will explore the role of individual courage in fostering collective courage and explore what community courage might look like in an educational context. Drawing from the works of Brown, Fullan,[23] and Heifetz and others we will delve into the relationship between individual and collective courage and the potential for transformational change in education.

Brown contends that individual courage is a prerequisite for fostering collective courage in organizations, and this becomes a catalyst for change. She posits that courageous leaders who embrace vulnerability, risk-taking, and accountability can inspire others to act with similar courage. This collective courage empowers communities to address systemic challenges, promote inclusivity, and drive innovation within educational settings.

According to Fullan, courageous leadership is critical for driving transformative change in education. He argues that individuals who demonstrate moral courage, resilience, and conviction can inspire others to work collaboratively toward shared goals and objectives. This collective action can facilitate transformative change by fostering a culture of continuous improvement, shared accountability, and collective efficacy.

Heifetz, Grashow, and Linsky's concept of adaptive leadership further highlights the importance of courageous leadership in fostering collective courage in an educational context. They argue that adaptive leaders can inspire others to confront complex, systemic issues by cultivating a culture of learning, innovation, and collaboration.

Collective courage in education might manifest as educators working together to address systemic inequities and ensure that all students have access to high-quality educational opportunities. This shared commitment to equitable education can result in transformative change at the community level.

Individual courageous leadership is necessary for fostering transformational change on a community scale in education. By embracing vulnerability, resilience, and conviction, courageous leaders can inspire collective courage, empowering communities to address systemic challenges, foster inclusivity, and drive innovation. Drawing from the insights from the previous sections, it is clear that individual courage is the catalyst for collective courage in education, ultimately leading to transformative change at the community level.

THE IMPORTANCE OF POLICY IN SHAPING CULTURE: THE ROLE OF SCHOOL BOARDS

Fostering courageous leadership in policymaking is born from equal parts leadership and culture. The focus of this book has been on building the supportive systemic structures that make for a granite foundation on which we can build great schools. Courageous policymaking leadership comes late in the framework because we have been slowly building our capacity for this type of leadership. As stated at the introduction of this chapter, courage can easily get you into problems, but it takes a different kind of courage to get you out of problems. Courageous policymaking is not for the faint of heart.

Policy in the field of education refers to the principles, guidelines, and regulations that govern the operation of educational institutions, as well as the allocation of resources and the establishment of priorities within these institutions. Policies are designed to shape the goals, values, and practices that underpin a school's culture, ensuring that the institution adheres to legal requirements and serves the needs of its students and the wider community. This section aims to discuss the importance of policy in the context of education and the critical role of school boards in adopting and implementing policies that shape the culture of a school or school district. We will also examine some examples of courageous policymaking and the implications for school districts.

To put it bluntly, policy is a foundation for educational culture. Policies play a significant role in shaping the culture of educational institutions. Policy is also bidirectional. Local climate begets culture over time, and culture begets policy. Many of our policies are written as a response to culture (take dress code policies as an example). Over time, however, the adoption and implementation of policies also determine the priorities, values, and practices that characterize a school's culture. Policies are instrumental in establishing the norms and expectations that define the relationships among students, teachers, administrators, and other stakeholders. For example, policies related to student behavior and discipline can create a culture of respect, responsibility, and accountability, while policies on curriculum and assessment can foster a culture of academic rigor, critical thinking, and intellectual curiosity. Educational policy is interesting in that it both influences and is influenced by the culture. This may not make intuitive sense at first but becomes understandable when we also realize educational systems are responsive to the local community but also responsible for building our next generation that creates society. Policy is the organization's way of accepting this reality. Courageous policymaking then is always forward looking and culture creating.

The importance of policy in shaping educational culture can be further understood by examining the ways in which policy affects various aspects of the school environment.

- Curriculum and Instruction: Educational policies establish the framework for curriculum development and instructional practices, ensuring that schools provide a comprehensive and well-rounded education that caters to the diverse needs of students. This includes policies on course offerings, instructional methods, and assessment practices.
- Equity and Inclusion: Policies aimed at promoting equity and inclusion address disparities in educational opportunities and outcomes among students of different backgrounds, ensuring that all students have equal access to quality education. These policies may include initiatives related to special education, language instruction, and cultural competency, among others.
- Student Services and Supports: Policies related to student services and supports ensure that schools provide the necessary resources and interventions to help students succeed academically, socially, and emotionally. This may include policies on counseling, extracurricular activities, and mental health services.
- School Governance and Accountability: Policies related to governance and accountability guide the decision-making processes within schools and school districts, ensuring transparency, consistency, and effectiveness in the administration of educational institutions. This includes policies on school board operations, budgeting, and performance evaluation.

As the governing bodies responsible for overseeing the administration and management of public schools, school boards play a critical role in the adoption and implementation of educational policies. School boards are typically composed of elected or appointed members who represent the interests of their local community. Their primary responsibilities include setting the strategic direction for the school district, establishing priorities and goals, and ensuring that the needs and expectations of students, parents, and the community are met.

In their capacity as policymakers, school boards must carefully consider the potential impact of policy decisions on the culture of the schools they govern. By adopting policies that promote student-centered, inclusive, and equitable learning environments, school boards can foster a culture that encourages student achievement, well-being, and personal growth. This requires ongoing engagement with various stakeholders, such as teachers, parents, and community members, to ensure that policies reflect the unique needs and aspirations of the local community.

Policy is a crucial component of the educational landscape, serving as the foundation on which school culture is built. The importance of policy in shaping the culture of educational institutions cannot be overstated because it determines the values, norms, and practices that guide the daily interactions and experiences of students, teachers, and administrators. As the governing bodies responsible for policy adoption and implementation, school boards play a pivotal role in creating and sustaining a positive and nurturing educational environment that promotes student achievement and well-being.

By understanding the significance of policy in shaping educational culture, school boards can make informed decisions that prioritize the needs and aspirations of their community. Through the thoughtful adoption of policies that promote equity, inclusion, and excellence, school boards can ensure that their schools become places where students thrive academically, socially, and emotionally. In this way, policy serves as a powerful tool for fostering a culture of learning, growth, and success in the field of education.

POLICY SCENARIO: OPEN ENROLLMENT

A school board in a diverse and economically divided district is considering an open enrollment policy to ensure greater access to a high-quality school or specialized program within the district. The aim is to provide students from lower-income neighborhoods, who may not have had access to the same level of resources and opportunities, with a chance to attend a school or program that would otherwise be beyond their reach. Implementing this policy would require courageous leadership and policymaking from the school board.

The school board would need to engage in courageous policymaking for several reasons:

- Addressing systemic inequities: Open enrollment policies challenge long-standing patterns of educational inequity rooted in factors such as socioeconomic status, race, and geography. Implementing this policy would require the school board to confront these systemic issues head-on, acknowledging their existence and working to dismantle them.
- Overcoming resistance: Open enrollment policies can be controversial and may face opposition from various stakeholders, including parents, teachers, and community members who may fear that opening

enrollment would lead to overcrowded schools, diminished resources, or lowered academic standards. The school board must be prepared to address these concerns and demonstrate the potential benefits of the policy, such as improved student outcomes, increased diversity, and more equitable access to educational opportunities.
- Navigating logistical challenges: Implementing an open enrollment policy involves managing complex logistical challenges, such as transportation, capacity planning, and resource allocation. The school board would need to develop a comprehensive plan for addressing these issues, ensuring that schools and programs have the necessary resources to accommodate incoming students.
- Ensuring transparency and fairness: The school board must develop a transparent and fair process for admitting students under the open enrollment policy. This may involve creating a lottery system, establishing admission criteria, or implementing a weighted lottery that prioritizes students based on factors such as socioeconomic status or proximity to the school. The school board must also be prepared to monitor the policy's impact on student outcomes and make adjustments as needed to ensure its effectiveness and fairness.

Examples of courageous leadership difficulties in the context of a larger community:

- Balancing competing interests: In a diverse community, the school board must balance the interests of various stakeholders, including parents, teachers, administrators, and students. This may involve making difficult decisions that may not please everyone, such as reallocating resources from wealthier schools to support lower-income students or prioritizing access for historically underserved populations.
- Facing public scrutiny and criticism: Courageous leadership often entails making unpopular decisions that may provoke backlash from community members who oppose the policy. The school board must be prepared to face public scrutiny and criticism, standing firm in their commitment to promoting equity and access for all students.
- Building consensus and trust: Implementing a significant policy change, such as open enrollment, requires building consensus and trust among stakeholders. The school board must engage in open dialogue with the community, addressing concerns and soliciting feedback to ensure that the policy is responsive to the needs and aspirations of all students and families.

Implementing an open enrollment policy in a diverse and economically divided district demands courageous leadership and policymaking from the school board. By confronting systemic inequities, overcoming resistance, navigating logistical challenges, and ensuring transparency and fairness, the school board can help create a more equitable and inclusive educational environment that benefits all students.

POLICY SCENARIO: WEIGHED LOTTERY

A school board in a diverse district with a history of educational disparities among different socioeconomic and racial groups is considering enacting a policy related to a weighted lottery system. This system is designed to ensure that historically underrepresented students have greater access to high-quality educational programming, thereby creating a more equitable educational landscape. Implementing this policy would require courageous leadership and policymaking from the school board.

The school board would need to engage in courageous policymaking for several reasons:

- Addressing historical inequities: A weighted lottery system directly addresses long-standing patterns of educational disparities and seeks to level the playing field for historically underrepresented students. The school board would need to confront these issues head-on, recognizing the need for targeted interventions to promote equity and access.
- Overcoming resistance: The introduction of a weighted lottery system may face opposition from various stakeholders, including parents, teachers, and community members who may perceive the policy as unfairly favoring certain groups over others. The school board must be prepared to address these concerns and articulate the rationale for the policy, emphasizing its goal of promoting equity and creating a more inclusive educational environment.
- Navigating logistical challenges: Implementing a weighted lottery system involves managing complex logistical challenges, such as defining the criteria for prioritizing students, ensuring the transparency and fairness of the lottery process, and monitoring the impact of the policy on student outcomes. The school board would need to develop a comprehensive plan for addressing these issues, ensuring that the policy is implemented effectively and equitably.
- Fostering community engagement and support: The success of a weighted lottery system depends on the support and engagement of the broader community, including parents, teachers, and students. The

school board must engage in open dialogue with stakeholders, addressing concerns, and soliciting feedback to ensure that the policy is responsive to the needs and aspirations of the community.

Examples of courageous leadership difficulties in the context of a larger community:

- Balancing competing interests: In a diverse community, the school board must balance the interests of various stakeholders, including those who may not directly benefit from the weighted lottery system. This may involve making difficult decisions and defending the policy's focus on promoting equity for historically underrepresented students.
- Facing public scrutiny and criticism: Courageous leadership often entails making unpopular decisions that may provoke backlash from community members who oppose the policy. The school board must be prepared to face public scrutiny and criticism, standing firm in their commitment to promoting equity and access for all students.
- Building consensus and trust: Implementing a significant policy change, such as a weighted lottery system, requires building consensus and trust among stakeholders. The school board must engage in open dialogue with the community, addressing concerns, and soliciting feedback to ensure that the policy is responsive to the needs and aspirations of all students and families.

Implementing a weighted lottery system to promote greater equity and access for historically underrepresented students demands courageous leadership and policymaking from the school board. By confronting historical inequities, overcoming resistance, navigating logistical challenges, and fostering community engagement and support, the school board can help create a more equitable and inclusive educational environment that benefits all students.

THE IMPACT OF COURAGEOUS LEADERSHIP AND POLICYMAKING

Courageous leadership and policymaking in education have long been recognized as crucial drivers of student success.[24] As the education landscape continues to evolve, courageous leaders and policymakers must be willing to make bold decisions to improve learning outcomes for all students. As in previous chapters, the following themes serve as the foundation for understanding the impact of courageous leadership and policymaking on student outcomes: continuous improvement, trust, enhanced communication, better decision-making, and maintaining a culture of improvement.

It is clear that courageous leadership and policymaking in education are essential for fostering a culture of continuous improvement.[25] When leaders and policymakers are committed to ongoing reflection, evaluation, and adaptation, schools are better equipped to respond to the changing needs of students, teachers, and the community. Continuous improvement enables educational institutions to evolve, ensuring that they remain relevant and effective in their pursuit of improved student outcomes.[26]

Trust is a critical component in the relationship between courageous leadership, policymaking, and student outcomes.[27] When leaders and policymakers demonstrate a commitment to transparency, honesty, and shared decision-making, trust is fostered among all stakeholders. This trust, in turn, leads to increased engagement, collaboration, and ultimately, improved student outcomes.[28]

Effective communication is a cornerstone of courageous leadership and policymaking in education. By fostering open lines of communication among all stakeholders, leaders and policymakers can better understand the needs and concerns of their community. Enhanced communication enables educational institutions to make more informed decisions, which ultimately leads to improved student outcomes.[29] It is paramount to remember that effective communication is a two-way street. A district must be as aggressive in soliciting input as they are in sharing information. A regular cadence of conversation with a broader community cannot be understated.

Courageous leadership and policymaking in education require the ability to make difficult decisions that may not always be popular.[30] By embracing a commitment to evidence-based decision-making and focusing on the best interests of students, leaders and policymakers can ensure that their choices drive positive student outcomes.[31]

Creating a culture of improvement requires ongoing dedication from leaders and policymakers.[32] By nurturing a growth mindset among all stakeholders, educational institutions can continually adapt and evolve to meet the needs of their students. This sustained focus on improvement is vital for ensuring long-term success and positive student outcomes.[33] We hearken back to a point made in this chapter: board policy is bidirectional in that it both responds to and creates culture.

Courageous leadership and policymaking in education play a critical role in driving improved student outcomes. By focusing on continuous improvement, trust, enhanced communication, better decision-making, and maintaining a culture of improvement, leaders and policymakers can create a transformative educational environment that fosters success for all students.

NOTES

1. Kotter, *Leading Change* (1996).
2. Heifetz, Grashow, and Linsky, *The Practice of Adaptive Leadership*.
3. Kanter, "The Ten Commandments of Change Management."
4. Brown, *Dare to Lead*.
5. Heifetz, Grashow, and Linsky, *The Practice of Adaptive Leadership*.
6. Kanter, "The Ten Commandments of Change Management."
7. Fullan, *Leading in a Culture of Change*.
8. Fullan, *Leading in a Culture of Change*.
9. Heifetz, Grashow, and Linsky, *The Practice of Adaptive Leadership*.
10. Fullan, *Leading in a Culture of Change*.
11. Kanter, "The Ten Commandments of Change Management."
12. Fullan, *The New Meaning of Educational Change*, 4th ed.
13. Rost, *Leadership for the Twenty-First Century*.
14. Shepherd, *The Secret to Transformational Leadership*.
15. Brown, *Dare to Lead*.
16. Nieto, *The Light in Their Eyes*.
17. Shepherd, *The Secret to Transformational Leadership*.
18. Jennings and Greenberg, "The Prosocial Classroom."
19. Deci and Ryan, "The 'What' and 'Why' of Goal Pursuits."
20. Shepherd, *The Secret to Transformational Leadership*.
21. Palmer, *The Courage to Teach*.
22. Heifetz, Grashow, and Linsky, *The Practice of Adaptive Leadership*.
23. Fullan, *Leading in a Culture of Change* (2014).
24. Hargreaves and Fullan, *Professional Capital*.
25. Kotter, *Leading Change* (2012).
26. Bryk and Schneider, *Trust in Schools*.
27. Leithwood and Louis, *Linking Leadership to Student Learning*.
28. Fullan, *Leading in a Culture of Change* (2014).
29. Spillane, Reiser, and Reimer, "Policy Implementation and Cognition."
30. Fullan, *Leading in a Culture of Change* (2014).
31. Marzano, Waters, and McNulty, *School Leadership That Works*.
32. Hargreaves and Fullan, *Professional Capital*.
33. Kotter, "The 8-Step Process for Leading Change."

Chapter 5

Cultivate Public Will and Understanding for Transformation

In a broad context, *public will* refers to the collective desire, sentiment, and opinion of the general public toward a particular issue, policy, or decision. It is the expression of the majority's preferences, values, and expectations, as well as their willingness to act collectively to achieve a common goal.

When it comes to education, public will can have a significant impact on the direction and priorities of education policies, funding, and curriculum. The public's demand for high-quality education, accessibility, and affordability can shape the local political educational agenda and funding decisions. The public can also influence the content of the curriculum and the emphasis on specific subjects, such as STEM or arts education.

Additionally, public will can influence the way educators and schools operate. The public's demand for accountability and transparency can lead to increased scrutiny and evaluation of the performance of teachers and schools. It can also lead to the adoption of new teaching methodologies, such as project-based learning or personalized learning, that reflect the public's preferences for more student-centered and practical approaches to education.

Overall, public will plays a crucial role in shaping the direction and effectiveness of education policies, programs, and practices. Understanding and responding to the public's demands and expectations can lead to better educational outcomes for students and society as a whole. The focus of this chapter will be on harnessing the power of public will to support transformation.

THE ROLE OF PUBLIC WILL IN LOCAL EDUCATION

Public will, the collective sentiment of a community, plays a vital role in shaping the local educational landscape. It has the potential to preserve the status quo, which can either be culture preserving or impeding of progress and reinforcing inequalities. Public will can also be a force for change, driving innovation and improvements in education.[1] This section examines the dual nature of public will in local education, discussing how it shapes and guides the status quo, as well as its transformative potential.

Public will and the status quo can be inextricably linked. Public will is a product of prevailing attitudes, values, and beliefs of a community, which can contribute to the perpetuation of existing structures and practices in education.[2] This is not necessarily a bad thing, as it can be culture preserving and culture perpetuating. This can be observed in how public will is often resistant to changes in education policy, such as school funding, curriculum, or assessment methods, especially when these changes challenge traditional norms and values.

In some cases, public will can maintain the status quo in a negative way by privileging certain groups and reinforcing educational inequalities. For instance, Lubienski and Lubienski[3] argue that public will contributes to the persistence of school segregation, as communities are resistant to policies aimed at promoting diversity and integration. Similarly, public will can reinforce economic disparities in education funding because wealthier communities often resist efforts to redistribute resources more equitably.[4]

However, public will can be a force for transformation. Despite its potential to uphold the status quo, public will can also be a powerful agent of change in local education. Community engagement and advocacy can contribute to policy shifts that address existing inequalities and promote improved educational outcomes.[5] For example, grassroots movements have successfully mobilized public will to advocate for changes in school funding formulas, leading to more equitable distribution of resources.[6]

Public will can also drive innovation in education, as communities demand new and improved methods of teaching and learning.[7] This can result in the adoption of alternative pedagogies, technological advancements, and curricular reforms that better meet the diverse needs of students.

Several factors shape and guide public will in local education. These include the influence of media and public discourse, which can both perpetuate and challenge prevailing attitudes toward education.[8] Additionally, the role of key stakeholders, such as educators, parents, and policymakers, is crucial in mobilizing public will for change.[9]

Moreover, research indicates that public will is more likely to support change when reforms are framed in terms of widely shared values, such as equity, opportunity, and excellence.[10] By connecting reforms to these values, advocates can build a broader consensus for change, thereby increasing the likelihood that public will becomes a force for transformation.

Public will plays a multifaceted, complex, and influential role in local education, as it can both uphold the status quo and drive transformation. Factors such as media, public discourse, and key stakeholders shape and guide public will, which can be harnessed to promote positive change in education. By understanding the dual nature of public will and the factors that influence it, policymakers, educators, and community members can better engage with public sentiment and work together to create more equitable and effective education systems.

WHY IS PUBLIC WILL IMPORTANT FOR TRANSFORMATION IN EDUCATION?

As we have learned, public will refers to the collective willingness and readiness of individuals to support and promote change initiatives. In education, garnering public will is crucial in driving and sustaining transformational efforts.[11] This section explores why public will is important in education transformation, highlighting the need for both initial support and sustained support over time. The consequences of lacking public will in transformational efforts are also discussed. Finally, the significance of public will in effecting change in the public sphere, be it in politics, community, or education, will be briefly examined.

Garnering public will is important in education transformation for various reasons. First, it ensures that changes are made with the backing of stakeholders. Public will is built on the understanding that change is necessary and that the proposed changes will improve the educational outcomes. When there is public will to transform education, stakeholders become invested in the change process, and they are more likely to contribute their resources, ideas, and expertise to the effort.[12]

Second, public will enables education transformation to gain traction and momentum. When the public is on board, the initiative gains visibility, and more individuals become interested in joining the cause. This makes it easier to mobilize support and resources, which are vital in achieving the desired changes. The momentum that public will creates can help to overcome resistance to change, especially from entrenched interests that may not want to see change happen.

Not only is public will important for initiating change, but it is critical in sustaining education transformation over time as well. Transforming education is a long-term process that requires continuous effort, investment, and innovation. Public will can help to ensure that the transformational efforts are sustained, even when there are setbacks or obstacles. Public will can be built through ongoing communication and engagement with stakeholders, which can help to keep them invested in the transformational efforts.[13]

The consequences of lacking public will in education transformation can be severe. Without public will, change efforts are likely to stall, and progress will be slow, if any. Lacking public will can also lead to resistance to change from stakeholders who feel that their voices are not being heard or that their concerns are being ignored, and hence, the reason for building an ownership culture early. Resistance can lead to a lack of buy-in, engagement, and ownership, which can make it difficult to achieve the desired changes.

Furthermore, the absence of public will can make it difficult to secure resources needed to drive the transformational efforts. Funding for education transformation often comes from public sources, such as taxes, and without public will, it can be challenging to secure the necessary funding to implement changes. This lack of funding can further hinder progress and make it difficult to achieve the desired outcomes. In this regard, the framework of this book becomes self-reinforcing, which leads to an ever-firmer foundation.

There is significance of public will in effecting change in the public sphere that is somewhat different from the private sphere. Public will is essential for effecting change in the public sphere, including in education, politics, and community initiatives. Public will provides the impetus for change and ensures that changes are made with the support of the people they will affect. In politics, public will is essential in shaping policy decisions because policymakers must consider the views and interests of their constituents.

In community initiatives, public will is critical in achieving social and economic changes that benefit the community as a whole. For instance, community projects such as the establishment of community centers, affordable housing, or community gardens require the support of community members to succeed. In education, public will is essential in driving and sustaining transformational efforts that can improve the quality of education and benefit the students, teachers, and the broader community.

Garnering public will is crucial in education transformation because it enables changes to be made with the backing of stakeholders, creates momentum and traction, and ensures the sustainability of the transformational efforts over time. Lacking public will can lead to resistance to change, a lack of resources, and slow progress, which can impede the achievement of desired educational outcomes. Finally, policymakers, educators, and community leaders must prioritize building public will in their transformational efforts to ensure that changes are made with the support of the people they affect.

THE ROLE OF THE SCHOOL BOARD MEMBER IN SHAPING PUBLIC WILL

Public school board members play a critical role in shaping the education system within their communities. They are tasked with making decisions that impact students' academic performance, school culture, and overall educational experience. To bring about change and transformation within public schools, it is important for board members to build and maintain public will. This section will explore specific strategies that public school board members can employ within their communities to build and maintain public will for change and transformation.

One of the most effective strategies for building and maintaining public will is to engage in open and transparent communication and do so early. Board members should be transparent about their decision-making process, provide regular updates on important issues, and actively seek out feedback from the community. By doing so, they can build trust and credibility with the public, which is essential for building support for change and transformation.

For example, in 2016,[14] the school board in Madison, Wisconsin, held a series of public meetings to discuss a proposal to change school start times. The board members were transparent about their rationale for the proposal, presented data and research to support their decision, and actively solicited feedback from parents, students, and teachers. As a result of this open and transparent communication, the board was able to build public support for the change, and the proposal was ultimately adopted.

Another effective strategy for building and maintaining public will is to collaborate with community stakeholders. Board members should work with parents, teachers, students, and community leaders to identify shared goals and priorities and to develop strategies for achieving them. By working collaboratively, board members can build a sense of ownership and investment in the education system within the community, which can help build support for change and transformation.

For example, in 2018, the school board in Guilford County, North Carolina,[15] collaborated with community stakeholders to develop a strategic plan for improving student outcomes. The board worked with parents, teachers, students, and community leaders to identify key priorities, such as increasing graduation rates and reducing achievement gaps, and to develop strategies for achieving these goals. By collaborating with community stakeholders, the board was able to build public support for the plan, which was ultimately adopted.

A third effective strategy for building and maintaining public will is to use data to inform decision-making. Board members should regularly collect and analyze data on student performance, school climate, and other important indicators to inform their decision-making process. By using data to make informed decisions, board members can build credibility with the public and demonstrate that they are committed to improving educational outcomes.

For example, in 2019, the school board in Montgomery County, Maryland,[16] used data to inform their decision to adopt a new mathematics curriculum. The board analyzed data on student performance, teacher feedback, and best practices in mathematics education to identify the strengths and weaknesses of the existing curriculum and to develop a plan for improvement. By using data to inform their decision-making, the board was able to build public support for the change, which was ultimately adopted.

Finally, board members should be responsive to community needs. They should actively seek out feedback from the community and adjust their decision-making process to meet the needs of the community. By being responsive to community needs, board members can build trust and credibility with the public and demonstrate that they are committed to improving educational outcomes.

As an example, in 2020, the school board in Seattle, Washington,[17] was faced with the challenge of providing distance learning to students during the COVID-19 pandemic. The board actively sought feedback from parents, teachers, and students and adjusted their decision-making process to meet the needs of the community. They provided technology and internet access to students who needed it, adjusted schedules to accommodate working parents, and provided mental health resources to support students and families. By being responsive to community needs, the board was able to build public support for their efforts to provide quality education during a difficult time.

In conclusion, building and maintaining public will is critical for bringing about change and transformation within public schools. Public school board members can employ a variety of strategies to build public will, including engaging in open and transparent communication, collaborating with community stakeholders, using data to inform decision-making, and being responsive to community needs. By employing these strategies, board members can build trust and credibility with the public, demonstrate their commitment to improving educational outcomes, and ultimately bring about positive change within their communities.

THE ROLE OF THE SUPERINTENDENT IN SHAPING PUBLIC WILL

Public school superintendents are responsible for overseeing the educational outcomes of students in their districts. They are also responsible for building and maintaining public will for change and transformation. To achieve this goal, superintendents need to develop specific strategies that work in tandem with school boards to address the needs and concerns of the community.[18] This section will explore effective strategies that public school superintendents can use to build and maintain public will for change and transformation. The strategies will be examined in the context of a self-reinforcing loop of transparency and trust with the public school board.

Strategy 1: Establishing Open Communication Channels. One effective strategy that superintendents can use to build public will for change and transformation is to establish open communication channels with the community. According to the National School Public Relations Association (NSPRA), communication is a critical component of building public support for schools.[19] By establishing open communication channels, superintendents can gain valuable feedback from the community on important issues that affect students, teachers, and parents.

One way to establish open communication channels is to hold regular town hall meetings. These meetings provide an opportunity for the superintendent to meet with community members and hear their concerns. Town hall meetings can also be used to provide updates on important initiatives and to solicit feedback from the community.

Another way to establish open communication channels is to maintain a strong social media presence. Social media platforms like Facebook, Twitter, and Instagram can be used to provide updates on important initiatives, share success stories, and solicit feedback from the community. A strong social media presence can also help to build trust between the superintendent and the community.

Strategy 2: Engaging Community Partnerships. Another effective strategy that superintendents can use to build public will for change and transformation is to engage community partnerships. According to the National School Boards Association (NSBA), community partnerships can help to build support for schools by demonstrating a shared commitment to the success of students.[20] By partnering with local businesses, nonprofit organizations, and community leaders, superintendents can build strong relationships with the community.

One way to engage community partnerships is to establish a community advisory board. This board can be composed of local business leaders, nonprofit organizations, and community leaders. The advisory board can provide valuable feedback on important initiatives and help to build support for schools within the community.

Another way to engage community partnerships is to establish a volunteer program. Volunteers can be recruited from the community to provide support for schools in a variety of ways, such as tutoring, mentoring, and fundraising. By engaging volunteers, superintendents can build strong relationships with the community and demonstrate a commitment to the success of students.

Strategy 3: Focusing on Student Achievement. A third effective strategy that superintendents can use to build public will for change and transformation is to focus on student achievement. According to the NSBA, student achievement is a critical component of building public support for schools.[21] By focusing on student achievement, superintendents can demonstrate a commitment to the success of students and build trust with the community.

One way to focus on student achievement is to establish a data-driven decision-making process. By collecting and analyzing data on student performance, superintendents can identify areas for improvement and develop strategies to address them. This data-driven approach can help to build trust with the community by demonstrating a commitment to transparency and accountability.

Another way to focus on student achievement is to celebrate success stories. By sharing stories of student success, superintendents can build support for schools within the community. Success stories can be shared through social media, local newspapers, and other communication channels.

Public school superintendents play a critical role in building and maintaining public will for change and transformation. To do this effectively, they need to develop strategies that address the needs and concerns of the community. Three effective strategies include establishing open communication channels, engaging community partnerships, and focusing on student achievement. These strategies can be used in a self-reinforcing loop of transparency and trust with the public school board, which can lead to increased support for schools within the community. By implementing these strategies, superintendents can build and maintain trust with the community, demonstrate a commitment to the success of students, and ultimately improve educational outcomes for all students in their district.

HOW A SUPERINTENDENT AND SCHOOL BOARD WORK TOGETHER TO SHAPE PUBLIC WILL

If public will is absent, it is highly likely a step in the framework described in this book has been missed along the way. To collectively shape public will, a collaborative approach between school district superintendents and boards of education is critical. This relationship is dynamic and ever evolving. In the sphere of public education, the collaboration between a public school district superintendent and a publicly elected board of education is crucial to shaping public will and effectively implementing policies that benefit students, teachers, and the community at large.[22] The interdependent nature of their roles demands a mutual understanding and commitment to work together in the pursuit of common goals. Let's explore this collaborative relationship, with a focus on deep listening, community engagement, deliberation of various perspectives, guidance from the superintendent, clear communication, speaking with one voice, and conducting business publicly and transparently.

The first priority is listening deeply to each other. Effective collaboration between the superintendent and the board of education requires a commitment to listening deeply to each other's ideas, concerns, and perspectives. Active listening helps to build trust, mutual respect, and understanding, which are essential for a productive working relationship. By acknowledging each other's expertise and valuing each other's unique insights, the superintendent and board members can better align their goals and strategies for shaping public will.

Engaging with the community is another key indicator. Both the superintendent and the board of education must prioritize engaging with their community to understand the needs, desires, and concerns of those they serve.

By actively participating in community events, hosting forums, and seeking input from diverse stakeholders, they demonstrate a commitment to being responsive and accountable to the public. The insights gained from these engagements can help shape policy decisions and ensure that the public's voice is represented in the decision-making process.

After engaging with the community, it is crucial for the superintendent and board members to share what they have learned with each other. This process allows them to identify common themes, areas of concern, and opportunities for growth. By collectively reflecting on community feedback, the superintendent and the board can better incorporate the public's perspective into their decision-making and develop strategies that truly represent the community's best interests.

As representatives of the public, board members must consider and sometimes deliberate a variety of perspectives when making decisions. Deliberation involves weighing the merits of different viewpoints, seeking to understand the underlying values and assumptions, and recognizing the potential consequences of their choices. This collaborative decision-making process ensures that the board's actions are informed by diverse perspectives and that they are responsive to the needs of their constituents.

Great boards also seek guidance from the superintendent. In their role as educational leaders, superintendents possess extensive knowledge of the organizational implications of potential decisions. As such, they can provide valuable guidance to the board in understanding the practical implications of policies and strategies. By seeking the superintendent's insights, board members can make more informed decisions that balance community desires with organizational realities.

It cannot be overstated how important it is to communicate clearly from the board table. Clear communication between the superintendent and the board is essential for ensuring that both parties understand their respective roles and responsibilities. By establishing open lines of communication, they can effectively collaborate, share information, and coordinate their efforts to shape public will.

After the conversation (and possibly a vote) at the board table, although board members may have differing opinions on particular issues, it is essential that they present a unified front when communicating decisions to the public. By speaking with "one voice," the board demonstrates its commitment to working together in the best interest of the community, even when there is dissent on a vote. This approach fosters trust and confidence in the board's ability to make difficult decisions on behalf of the public.

It goes without saying the board must conduct business publicly and transparently. To ensure the community's trust and support, the superintendent and the board of education must conduct their business publicly and transparently.

This means making information about meetings, decision-making processes, and outcomes readily accessible to the public. By conducting their work in an open and transparent manner, the superintendent and board demonstrate their commitment to accountability, which is essential for fostering public confidence in their ability to shape public will.

Shaping public will requires a collaborative approach between the public school district superintendent and the publicly elected board of education. Through deep listening, community engagement, open deliberation, seeking guidance from the superintendent, clear communication, speaking with one voice, and conducting business publicly and transparently, these educational leaders can effectively navigate the challenges of public education and develop policies and strategies that best serve the needs of their community. This collaboration is essential for building trust, promoting accountability, and fostering a responsive and effective educational system that benefits all stakeholders.

SUMMING IT UP

Transforming the core of learning in public school districts requires systemic changes that support and sustain the transformation. In this section, I will review that establishing equitable funding structures, developing quality assurance frameworks, fostering community-wide ownership of learning, cultivating courageous leadership and policymaking, and cultivating public will and understanding for transformation are crucial steps in supporting transformative change.

Transforming the core of learning in public school districts is important work that should be happening right now because it is necessary to ensure that all students have access to high-quality education. The current education system in many public school districts perpetuates disparities in educational outcomes based on race, income, and zip code. This perpetuation of disparities is both unacceptable and unjust. Transformative change is necessary to address these disparities and ensure that all students have an equal opportunity to succeed. And this takes leadership courage.

Step 1: Establish Equitable Funding Structures. Equitable funding structures are crucial for identifying areas of transformation in public school districts. Schools in low-income neighborhoods often receive less funding than schools in affluent neighborhoods, which leads to disparities in educational outcomes.[23] By establishing equitable funding structures, school districts can identify areas where resources need to be allocated to improve educational outcomes for all students. This step is essential in creating a foundation for transformation because it ensures that all students have access to the resources needed to succeed.

Establishing equitable funding structures is important because it ensures that resources are allocated based on need and not zip code. When schools in low-income neighborhoods receive less funding, students in those neighborhoods are at a disadvantage. Equitable funding structures ensure that all students have access to the resources they need to succeed. Equitable funding structures are an antecedent to making programmatic decisions and determining the effectiveness of those programs, which is why the development of quality assurance frameworks is the next step.

Step 2: Develop Quality Assurance Frameworks. As a consequence of establishing equitable funding structures, school districts are then able to develop quality assurance frameworks to ensure that resources are being used effectively. Quality assurance frameworks provide a set of standards and criteria that schools can use to measure their performance and identify areas for improvement. This step helps build trust and transparency because it demonstrates a commitment to accountability and continuous improvement.

Developing quality assurance frameworks is important because it ensures that resources are being used effectively. Without quality assurance frameworks, there is a risk that resources will be wasted or misused. Quality assurance frameworks ensure that schools are accountable for their performance and that they are continuously improving. This is a necessary antecedent for what comes next, building a sense of community ownership around decision-making.

Step 3: Foster Community-Wide Ownership of Learning. Fostering community-wide ownership of learning is crucial in creating deeper trust, transparency, and commitment for change. This is much easier with equitable funding structures and quality assurance frameworks in place. When the community feels invested in the educational outcomes of students, they are more likely to support transformative change. This step involves engaging parents, community organizations, and local businesses in the educational process. By involving the community in the educational process, school districts can build stronger relationships with stakeholders and demonstrate a commitment to collaboration.

Fostering community-wide ownership of learning is important because it ensures that all stakeholders are invested in the educational outcomes of students. When the community is invested in the educational process, they are more likely to support transformative change. This support is crucial in sustaining the transformation over time. Transformation over time is a bellwether for the establishment of a group that is galvanized around long-term thinking, and this begets the next step, which is cultivating courageous leadership and policymaking.

Step 4: Cultivate Courageous Leadership and Policymaking. Cultivating courageous leadership and policymaking is essential in creating a self-reinforcing cycle of community support. School district leaders need to be willing to take risks and make difficult decisions to support transformative change. Policymakers also need to be willing to create policies that support transformation, even if they are not politically popular. This step is crucial in building trust and demonstrating a commitment to long-term change.

Cultivating courageous leadership and policymaking is important because it ensures that school district leaders and policymakers are willing to take risks and make difficult decisions to support transformative change. Without courageous leadership and policymaking, transformative change is unlikely to occur. Only with these first four steps in place, can we make the final step into cultivation of public will and understanding for transformation.

Step 5: Cultivate Public Will and Understanding for Transformation. Finally, cultivating public will and understanding for transformation is essential for sustaining the transformation. This step involves creating a narrative around the importance of transformative change and engaging the community in a dialogue about the benefits of change. By cultivating public will and understanding for transformation, school districts can create a supportive environment for change and ensure that the transformation is sustained over time.

Cultivating public will and understanding for transformation is important because it ensures that the transformation is sustained beyond the life of any one leader. Public will is the legacy we leave behind. Without public support, transformative change is unlikely to occur or be sustained. Cultivating public will and understanding for transformation ensures that the community is engaged in the educational process and is invested in the success of students.

Transforming the core of learning in public school districts requires systemic changes that support and sustain the transformation. By establishing equitable funding structures, developing quality assurance frameworks, fostering community-wide ownership of learning, cultivating courageous leadership and policymaking, and cultivating public will and understanding for transformation, school districts can create a framework and theory of action for supporting transformative change. This approach ensures that all students have access to the resources needed to succeed and creates a supportive environment for change. Ultimately, this approach leads to improved educational outcomes for all students in the district.

PUTTING IT TOGETHER

With the framework and theory of action in place, let us now turn our attention to a practical application and case study. In the second half of the book,

Transform the Core of Learning

Learning Structures
Enable development of diverse learning structures

Talent Development
Develop human capital around learning

Data & Digital Ecosystem
Develop a learner-focused infrastructure & ecosystem

Learning Culture
Create new personalized learning cultures

Assessment/Credentialing
Enable new forms of assessment & credentialing

Public Will
Cultivate public will & understanding for transformation

Transform Supporting Systemic Structures

Funding
Establish equitable funding structures around student learning

Leadership & Policy
Foster courageous leadership & policymaking

Community Ownership
Foster community-wide ownership of learning

Quality Assurance
Establish new quality assurance frameworks

we will specifically look at an initiative called "The Participatory Budgeting Project" launched in Victoria, Texas, in 2022. We will refer to the framework you've learned in this first part of the book and will describe the steps we took in using that framework as a theory of action (refer to the Introduction for a reminder about the difference between a framework and theory of action).

NOTES

1. Evans, "Public Will and Education Reform."
2. Kober, "Public Opinion and Education Policy."
3. Lubienski and Lubienski, *The Public School Advantage*.
4. Baker and Corcoran, "The Stealth Inequities of School Funding."
5. Evans, "Public Will and Education Reform."
6. Welner and Carter, *Closing the Opportunity Gap*.
7. Kober, "Public Opinion and Education Policy."
8. Evans, "Public Will and Education Reform."
9. Kober, "Public Opinion and Education Policy."
10. Welner and Carter, *Closing the Opportunity Gap*.
11. Chubb, "Why Public Will Is Crucial in Education Reform."
12. Darling-Hammond, Wilhoit, and Pittenger, "Accountability for College and Career Readiness."
13. Smyth, Down, McInerney, and Hattam, "School Community Partnerships in Neoliberal Times."
14. Madison Metropolitan School District, "High School Start Time Changes."
15. Guilford County Schools, "Strategic Plan."
16. Montgomery County Public Schools, "Math Program Review."
17. Seattle Public Schools, "COVID-19: Remote Learning."
18. National School Boards Association, "Building Community Support for Public Schools."
19. National School Public Relations Association, "Communication and Community Engagement."
20. National School Boards Association, "Building Community Support for Public Schools."
21. National School Boards Association, "Building Community Support for Public Schools."
22. National School Public Relations Association, "Communication and Community Engagement."
23. García and Weiss, "School Funding and Student Success: A Review of the Literature."

Chapter 6

Participatory Budgeting

Participatory budgeting (PB) is a democratic process that has been gaining traction worldwide over the past three decades for its potential to revolutionize the way communities allocate public resources. By directly involving citizens in the decision-making process, PB aims to create a more equitable and transparent distribution of funds, empowering local communities to take ownership of their priorities and needs. This chapter delves into the concept of PB, exploring its history, expansion across international boundaries, and its overall impact on democracy.

A BRIEF OVERVIEW OF PARTICIPATORY BUDGETING

PB emerged as an innovative approach to fiscal decision-making, driven by the belief that citizens should have a say in how public funds are spent.[1] In this process, citizens propose, discuss, and prioritize projects and initiatives for a portion of the public budget. Typically, the cycle begins with community members attending meetings to voice their concerns and identify pressing issues. These concerns are then translated into concrete proposals that are presented to the community for deliberation and voting. Once the votes are tallied, the winning projects are funded and implemented, with progress monitored by the community.

This model of budget allocation promotes transparency, accountability, and social inclusion. By involving citizens in the decision-making process, PB seeks to foster a sense of belonging and trust between government institutions and the communities they serve, ultimately strengthening the foundations of democracy. This should resonate with the first five chapters of this book.

The birth of PB can be traced back to 1989 in the city of Porto Alegre, Brazil.[2] As a response to the rampant corruption and inefficiency within the traditional budgeting process, the Workers' Party (PT) introduced PB as a means of restoring trust and promoting social justice. Initially confined to the local level, the experiment proved highly successful, leading to improved public services and greater citizen satisfaction. This aligns with the concept learned in chapter 1, "equitable funding structures."

The Porto Alegre model soon caught the attention of other municipalities in Brazil and abroad, prompting the expansion of PB throughout Latin America,[3] Europe, Africa, Asia, and North America. In 2004, PB made its debut in the United States with an initiative in Chicago. Over time, PB initiatives have adapted to the unique contexts and challenges of the cities and communities in which they are implemented, resulting in various models that share the core principles of direct citizen participation and democratic decision-making. This facilitates deep "ownership" as discussed in chapter 3.

The growth of PB across international boundaries has been fueled by a combination of factors, including the recognition of its potential to strengthen democracy, address social inequalities, and improve public services.[4] Further, social media and the internet facilitate a rapid spreading of ideas. Supranational organizations such as the United Nations and the World Bank have endorsed PB as a means of advancing good governance and local development.[5] Chapters 4 and 5 focused on creating a will for change and leadership courage.

One notable example of PB's international expansion is the European Union's adoption of the process as part of its cohesion policy,[6] aimed at reducing economic disparities among its member states. In the early 2000s, several European cities, such as Seville (Spain) and Berlin-Lichtenberg (Germany), began implementing PB initiatives to encourage civic engagement and improve the allocation of public resources.

In Africa, countries like Senegal, Kenya, and South Africa have employed PB as a tool for fostering local development, social justice, and transparency. Asia has also seen the growth of PB initiatives, with countries like India, China, and the Philippines incorporating the process into their governance structures to enhance local democracy.

As PB has spread across the globe, its impact on democracy has become increasingly evident. PB initiatives have been successful in fostering civic engagement and promoting accountability by empowering citizens to influence public spending directly. This inclusive approach to decision-making has facilitated greater transparency in the allocation of resources, addressing issues of corruption and inefficiency that often plague traditional budgeting processes. This is addressed in chapter 2, and the importance of creating "quality assurance frameworks."

Moreover, PB has played a significant role in promoting social inclusion by ensuring that historically marginalized and underrepresented groups have a greater voice in the decision-making process. By actively involving these groups, PB has facilitated a more equitable distribution of resources and enabled the prioritization of projects that address the specific needs of diverse communities.

The impact of PB on democracy goes beyond the immediate outcomes of the process itself. By fostering a culture of civic engagement, PB contributes to the development of an informed and active citizenry that is more likely to hold governments accountable and demand better public services. This heightened level of political participation is essential for the long-term health and sustainability of democratic systems.

Furthermore, the success of PB initiatives in enhancing trust between citizens and government institutions cannot be understated. As citizens see their input reflected in tangible improvements to their communities, their faith in the democratic process is strengthened, leading to a more resilient and robust democracy.

PB has emerged as a transformative force in the realm of democratic governance. By engaging citizens directly in the allocation of public resources, PB has revolutionized the way communities prioritize their needs and address social inequalities. With its roots in Porto Alegre, Brazil, PB has expanded across international boundaries, gaining recognition for its potential to enhance democracy, foster social inclusion, and improve public services. As the practice continues to evolve and adapts to diverse contexts, its impact on democracy will likely endure, shaping the future of civic engagement and participatory governance around the world.

PB is a democratic process in which community members (defined as you see fit) decide how to spend part of a public budget. It gives people real power over real money. This is related to the participatory policymaking process promoted by the advocacy group Democracy Beyond Elections,[1] which has made significant contributions to our thinking as it relates to spending in K–12 education. The five steps of PB are (1) design the process, (2) brainstorm ideas, (3) develop proposals, (4) vote, and (5) fund winning projects.

Designing the process involves a steering committee that represents the wider community. It is responsible for creating the engagement plan for the remaining steps. The second step, brainstorming, is an opportunity for the community to share ideas. This can be done in person or through crowdsourcing tools that are easily accessible.

Developing proposals in step 3 asks "budget delegates" to develop the ideas into feasible proposals for consideration. Budget delegates are people who can usher proposals from an idea into a plan. If a proposal came forward to put a smartboard in every classroom, the budget delegates would put pen to paper to figure out what the total cost would be from purchasing to implementation.

Because so many ideas will emerge, the work of the budget delegates is paramount. The ideas must be reviewed and developed by the steering committee. The full community votes on the proposals in step 4. The voting can range from simple ways, such as using a traditional ballot box, to more complicated ways involving crowdsourcing tools. By going through the process of voting, the community decides what is most important. Finally, in step 5, the organization funds the winning projects and begins implementation. It is straightforward, but planning is key.

As we move forward into the twenty-first century, the importance of participatory budgeting and its influence on democracy cannot be overstated. As more communities around the globe embrace this innovative approach to public decision-making, the potential for positive change in the relationship between citizens and their governments becomes increasingly apparent. The key to this transformation lies in the continued spread and refinement of PB initiatives, as well as in the cultivation of a culture that values civic engagement, transparency, and social justice.

The growth of PB also highlights the need for further research and evaluation of its impact and effectiveness. By examining the successes and challenges of PB initiatives in various contexts, practitioners and policymakers can gain valuable insights into how to tailor the process to the unique needs of their communities. This will be the focus of the next chapter. This, in turn, will ensure that PB remains a powerful tool for strengthening democracy and promoting equitable development for years to come.

PB has come a long way since its inception in Porto Alegre, Brazil. Its growth across international boundaries and the powerful impact it has had on democracy are testaments to the power of citizen engagement and the potential for innovative approaches to governance. As PB continues to evolve and adapt to new contexts, it remains an essential tool for nurturing the growth and development of democratic systems worldwide. By embracing the principles of transparency, inclusion, and collaboration, communities can work together to create a brighter future for all, built on the foundations of genuine civic participation and equitable resource allocation.

Let us delve deeper into the world of PB, examining its various models, methodologies, and case studies that highlight its successes and challenges. Hopefully, this exploration will create further interest and engagement in PB, encouraging its continued growth and evolution as a driving force for democratic innovation and progress.

CROSSING INTERNATIONAL BOUNDARIES: A JOURNEY OF DEMOCRATIC PRINCIPLES

PB has become a powerful tool for civic engagement and democratic innovation, with roots in Brazil and a growing presence in diverse regions around the world. This decentralized, bottom-up approach to allocating public funds has evolved to suit the unique cultural, social, and political contexts of each region, resulting in a range of PB models that share core principles while differing in implementation. This section examines the international history of PB in depth, tracing its expansion from Brazil to other countries, highlighting similarities and differences between these PB initiatives, and offering insights into the reasons behind these variations.

FROM BRAZIL TO THE WORLD: THE ORIGINS AND EXPANSION OF PARTICIPATORY BUDGETING

PB emerged in Porto Alegre, Brazil, in 1989 as an innovative approach to involve citizens in the allocation of public resources.[7] PT initiated the process in response to the long-standing problems of corruption, clientelism, and social inequality that plagued the city's governance).[8] By engaging residents in budgetary decision-making, the PT aimed to increase transparency, promote social justice, and enhance democratic accountability.

The Porto Alegre model of PB was designed to address three primary issues: (1) resource allocation that was disproportionately favoring wealthier neighborhoods, (2) a lack of transparency in public spending, and (3) low levels of citizen participation in political processes.[9] Through the PB process, citizens were empowered to identify, discuss, and prioritize local infrastructure and social projects, ultimately influencing how public funds were allocated.

The success of PB in Porto Alegre was evident in various ways. First, the process led to a more equitable distribution of resources, improving public services in historically marginalized neighborhoods. Second, PB fostered a sense of community and encouraged active citizenship by giving residents the opportunity to engage directly in decision-making processes. Lastly, the increased transparency and accountability in public spending resulted in higher levels of trust in local government and reduced corruption.

The positive outcomes of PB in Porto Alegre garnered international attention, inspiring the adoption of similar initiatives across Brazil, Latin America, and beyond. As the concept spread to Europe, Africa, Asia, and North America, it began to influence the political and cultural climate in various ways. PB has been credited with fostering a sense of civic engagement and social solidarity among participating communities.[10] Moreover, PB has been instrumental in promoting a culture of transparency and accountability in public administration, helping to dismantle corrupt practices and promote good governance.[11]

However, it is important to note that the success of PB initiatives in Brazil is contingent upon several factors, such as the degree of institutional support, local political culture, and the availability of resources.[12] As such, the impact of PB varies across contexts, with some instances resulting in transformative changes, while others face challenges in sustaining momentum and delivering on their promises.[13]

The advent of PB in Porto Alegre came as a response to pervasive corruption and social inequality. The initial and subsequent initiatives proved successful in promoting social justice, increasing citizen satisfaction, and enhancing political participation.

One of the key factors driving the international expansion of PB was its potential to strengthen democracy, address social inequalities, and improve public services.[14] Supranational organizations such as the United Nations and the World Bank have endorsed PB as a means of advancing good governance and local development.[15] In response, many countries have adopted and adapted the PB process to fit their unique contexts and challenges, resulting in a diverse array of models that differ in terms of scale, scope, and implementation.

REGIONAL VARIATIONS AND EVOLUTIONS OF PARTICIPATORY BUDGETING

In Latin America, the spread of PB has been closely tied to the region's broader push for decentralization and the strengthening of local governments.[16] Several countries, including Mexico, Peru, and Argentina, have implemented PB initiatives that focus on addressing social inequalities and promoting transparency in public spending. However, the degree of citizen participation and the allocation of resources for PB initiatives have varied widely across the region, reflecting differing political, social, and economic contexts.[17]

European PB initiatives have often emphasized the importance of civic engagement and the inclusion of marginalized populations in the decision-making process.[18] In the early 2000s, cities such as Seville (Spain) and Berlin-Lichtenberg (Germany) began implementing PB initiatives, adapting the process to their specific contexts and needs. In some cases, European PB initiatives have focused on specific sectors, such as youth, education, or the environment, while others have adopted a more comprehensive approach to public spending. The European Union's cohesion policy, aimed at reducing economic disparities among its member states, has also incorporated PB as a tool for fostering civic engagement and improving the allocation of public resources.[19]

In Africa, PB has emerged as a tool for fostering local development, social justice, and transparency, with countries such as Senegal, Kenya, and South Africa implementing PB initiatives. One notable example is the Kenyan experience, where PB has been integrated into the country's broader decentralization and devolution process, enabling local communities to directly participate in budgeting decisions. However, the implementation and success of PB initiatives in Africa have often been constrained by limited resources, weak institutional capacity, and political challenges.[20]

In Asia, PB initiatives have emerged in countries like India, China, and the Philippines, with a focus on enhancing local democracy and addressing social inequalities. In India, for example, the state of Kerala has integrated PB into its broader decentralization process, enabling citizens to directly participate in the allocation of development funds.[21] China, on the other hand, has experimented with PB in select cities as a means of increasing government transparency and fostering civic engagement, although the process remains relatively limited in scope and scale.[22]

SIMILARITIES AND DIFFERENCES: UNDERSTANDING THE EVOLUTION OF PARTICIPATORY BUDGETING INTERNATIONALLY

Despite the diverse contexts in which PB has been implemented, several similarities can be observed across international initiatives. These include a focus on promoting transparency, accountability, and social inclusion; the active involvement of citizens in the decision-making process; and the use of deliberative methods to facilitate dialogue and consensus-building among participants. Put simply, PB is a process that allows citizens to directly engage in the allocation of public resources.[23]

However, PB initiatives also differ significantly in terms of their scale, scope, and implementation, reflecting the unique political, social, and economic contexts of each region. Factors influencing these differences include the degree of decentralization and local autonomy, the availability of resources, the capacity of civil society organizations, and the political will to support and sustain PB initiatives.[24]

Several factors may explain the changes observed in PB as it has crossed international boundaries. First, the adaptation of PB to different contexts has often been driven by the need to address specific local challenges and priorities, such as social inequalities, corruption, or environmental concerns.[25] Second, the involvement of international organizations and donors has influenced the design and implementation of PB initiatives, with varying degrees of emphasis placed on aspects such as civic engagement, capacity-building, or institutional reform.[26] Finally, the diffusion of PB has been facilitated by networks of practitioners, researchers, and activists who have shared knowledge, experiences, and best practices across borders, contributing to the development of new models and approaches.

The international journey of PB highlights the adaptability and versatility of this democratic innovation, which has evolved to suit diverse contexts and challenges across the globe. Despite significant variations in implementation, PB initiatives worldwide share common goals of promoting transparency, accountability, and social inclusion, reflecting the enduring appeal of this approach to public decision-making. As PB continues to spread and adapt to new contexts, its potential to strengthen democracy, address social inequalities, and improve public services remains an essential area of exploration for scholars, practitioners, and policymakers alike.

The context and history of PB illustrates the capacity of this innovative approach to democratic governance to transcend international boundaries and adapt to diverse cultural, social, and political contexts. By examining the similarities and differences among PB initiatives across regions, as well as the factors driving these variations, we can gain valuable insights into the potential of PB to promote more inclusive, responsive, and transparent decision-making processes. As PB continues to evolve and expand globally, its impact on democracy, social justice, and public service provision remains an important area for further research, experimentation, and learning.

PARTICIPATORY BUDGETING AS A FORM OF DEMOCRACY

Democracy can be defined as a system of government in which citizens have the power to make decisions on public matters.[27] PB, as a democratic process, seeks to include citizens in the decision-making process by providing them with a platform to discuss, deliberate, and determine budgetary priorities.[28] This direct involvement of citizens in budgetary decisions embodies several key democratic principles, such as popular sovereignty, political equality, and deliberative decision-making.

Popular sovereignty, the principle that political power resides in the people, is at the core of PB.[29] By allowing citizens to participate in the allocation of public resources, PB recognizes the inherent right of individuals to have a say in the decisions that affect their lives and communities.

Political equality, the idea that all citizens have equal opportunities to influence public decisions, is also central to PB. The participatory nature of PB helps to reduce power imbalances and promote the inclusion of marginalized groups in the decision-making process.[30] By providing a platform for all citizens to voice their concerns and priorities, PB fosters a more equitable distribution of resources and services.

Deliberative decision-making, the process through which individuals engage in reasoned discussion and debate to arrive at collective decisions, is another key aspect of democracy that is embodied by PB.[31] Through structured deliberations, PB encourages citizens to consider different perspectives and collaborate to find solutions that benefit the broader community.

PB offers several benefits as a form of democratic governance, including increased civic engagement, improved public services, and enhanced social justice. By involving citizens in the decision-making process, PB fosters a sense of ownership and responsibility, leading to higher levels of civic engagement.[32] This heightened engagement can contribute to the development of a more informed and active citizenry, which is essential for a healthy democracy.

Additionally, PB has been shown to result in more effective and responsive public services.[33] By incorporating the knowledge and preferences of citizens, PB can lead to better-targeted and more efficient allocation of resources, addressing the specific needs and priorities of local communities.

Furthermore, PB can contribute to enhanced social justice by promoting the equitable distribution of public resources and services. By prioritizing the needs of marginalized and underserved populations, PB can help to reduce disparities and foster greater social cohesion.

Despite its potential benefits, PB also faces several challenges. One major challenge is the potential for elite capture, where powerful groups or individuals manipulate the process to serve their own interests. To mitigate this risk, it is crucial to establish transparent and accountable mechanisms that promote broad-based participation and prevent the undue influence of powerful actors.[34]

Another challenge is the limited scope and scale of PB initiatives, which often focus on small portions of municipal budgets.[35] Expanding the scope of PB to include larger shares of public budgets may enhance its potential impact and foster a more comprehensive understanding of public finances among citizens.

Lastly, the sustainability and institutionalization of PB initiatives can be hindered by political resistance and limited resources. Building strong partnerships among civil society organizations, local governments, and other stakeholders is essential for overcoming these challenges and ensuring the long-term success of PB initiatives.[36]

PB, as a form of democratic governance, embodies key principles of democracy, such as popular sovereignty, political equality, and deliberative decision-making. By fostering civic engagement, improving public services, and promoting social justice, PB offers a promising approach to enhancing democratic governance. However, it is crucial to address the challenges associated with PB, such as elite capture, limited scope, and sustainability issues, to fully realize its potential benefits. Further research is needed to explore innovative strategies and best practices for implementing PB in various contexts, ensuring its effectiveness and sustainability as a democratic tool.

PARTICIPATORY BUDGETING IN THE UNITED STATES: EXAMPLES AND OUTCOMES

We have established that PB is a democratic process allowing citizens to directly influence the allocation of public resources.[37] Since its inception, PB has spread to more than three thousand cities around the world.[38] In the United States, PB has gained traction in recent years as a means of enhancing civic engagement, promoting transparency, and addressing inequality in public spending.[39] This section will explore various examples of PB in the United States, analyzing the reasons for their implementation, their outcomes, and their potential for success.

Small-Scale PB Projects

- Chicago, Illinois: In 2009, Chicago became the first city in the United States to implement PB, led by Alderman Joe Moore of the 49th Ward.[40] Residents decided on how to allocate a portion of the ward's discretionary budget, called *menu money*, which was set at $1.3 million. This pilot project was successful in increasing civic engagement, as nearly one thousand residents participated in the process. The project funded various neighborhood improvements, including street resurfacing, sidewalk repairs, and streetlight installations.[41]
- Vallejo, California: In 2012, Vallejo became the first city in the United States to implement PB citywide.[42] Residents were given the power to decide on how to allocate $3.2 million in Measure B funds, a 1 percent sales tax increase approved by voters. More than four thousand residents participated in the process, which funded projects like street and sidewalk improvements, public safety initiatives, and park upgrades. The initiative was considered successful in promoting community engagement and collaboration.

Large-Scale PB Projects

- New York City: New York City is home to the largest PB initiative in the United States, with more than thirty city council districts participating

since 2011.[43] In 2019, the city allocated more than $40 million for PB projects, with residents deciding on projects ranging from park improvements to technology upgrades in schools. The New York City initiative has been praised for its scale, inclusivity, and focus on engaging marginalized communities.
- Seattle, Washington: In 2017, Seattle launched the Youth Voice, Youth Choice program, a PB initiative focused on engaging youth aged eleven to twenty-five.[44] The program allocated $2 million for youth-selected projects, including park improvements, cultural programs, and job training. The initiative was successful in engaging more than three thousand young people, particularly those from historically underrepresented communities.

This brief overview of PB initiatives in the United States demonstrates that PB has been implemented in various forms and scales across the country. Overall, PB initiatives have been successful in promoting civic engagement, fostering collaboration, and addressing local needs. However, some challenges have emerged in the implementation of PB initiatives. For instance, the process can be time-consuming and require considerable resources for organizing and facilitating. Additionally, there is a risk of unequal participation, with more affluent and educated citizens potentially dominating the process.[45]

Despite these challenges, PB holds promise as a means of enhancing democracy, transparency, and equity in public spending. Future research could explore strategies to mitigate potential pitfalls and expand the scope and impact of PB initiatives in the United States.

PARTICIPATORY BUDGETING IN EDUCATION: EMPOWERING COMMUNITIES AND FOSTERING DEMOCRACY

This section will examine the use of PB in public education in the United States, focusing on various case studies to highlight the outcomes and benefits of these projects. By providing a comprehensive understanding of the PB process in public education, this will contribute to the ongoing discourse on the importance of democratic decision-making and community empowerment in educational contexts. Similarities among the projects will be summarized, and the potential for future research and application will be suggested.

Case Study 1: Phoenix Union High School District, Arizona

The Phoenix Union High School District (PUHSD) in Arizona implemented PB in 2015, giving students, staff, and community members the opportunity to allocate a portion of the district's budget.[46] The process involved gathering ideas, developing proposals, and voting on projects. Outcomes of the PB initiative included the allocation of funds toward technology upgrades, campus improvements, and professional development for educators.

Case Study 2: New York City Public Schools

New York City has been a leader in implementing PB in public schools. In 2011, Council Member Brad Lander partnered with several community organizations to launch PB in four schools in his district.[47] The initiative expanded in 2014 when the New York City Council included ten schools in its citywide PB initiative.[48] Outcomes of these projects have included improved school facilities, expanded extracurricular activities, and the purchase of new technology and equipment for classrooms.

Case Study 3: Boston Public Schools

In 2014, Boston Public Schools launched a PB initiative called "Youth Lead the Change," which gave young people aged twelve to twenty-five the power to allocate $1 million of the city's capital budget.[49] The project aimed to engage youth in the budgeting process and promote civic participation. Outcomes included investments in school renovations, technology upgrades, and improvements to public spaces and recreational facilities.

To summarize, an analysis of PB initiatives in public education in the United States reveals several similarities. In each case, community members, including students, were given the opportunity to actively participate in the decision-making process. The outcomes of these projects have generally focused on improving the quality of education, upgrading school facilities, and promoting a sense of ownership and empowerment among participants. These findings suggest that PB can serve as an effective tool for promoting democratic decision-making and community engagement in public education.

WHERE DO WE GO FROM HERE?

The widespread adoption of PB in public education across the United States is a testament to its efficacy in engaging communities, empowering students and staff, and fostering democratic decision-making. As evidenced by the case studies presented here, PB initiatives have led to improved educational facilities, increased access to technology, and enhanced learning opportunities. Through the promotion of civic participation and shared decision-making, PB offers a promising avenue for strengthening public education systems and fostering positive outcomes for students and their communities.

By continuing to explore and expand on the principles and practices of PB, we can work toward a future in which democracy is truly inclusive, responsive, and reflective of the diverse voices that comprise our global community. PB stands as a testament to the transformative potential of citizen engagement and collaboration in the decision-making process. By fostering a sense of shared responsibility and ownership in public spending, PB has the power to create stronger, more resilient communities that are better equipped to tackle the complex challenges of the modern world.

Our country was founded on the principles of democracy. The cornerstones of our democracy include freedom of assembly, association and speech, inclusiveness and equality, citizenship and voting rights. We teach these ideals in class, but how often do we demonstrate them in our actions? Perhaps the best way to teach our students how to preserve and protect this great democracy is for leaders to live these principles in our actions. PB is a mechanism by which we can do this. The impact might be life-changing.

Future initiatives should continue to explore the impact of PB initiatives on educational outcomes and the potential for scaling these projects to reach more schools and communities across the United States. In the next chapter, you will be presented with a case study from Victoria, Texas. In this case study you will read about one of the largest PB projects undertaken by a school district on a system-wide scale. To ensure accuracy of detail, the project manager (Justin Gabrysch) was asked to author the chapter. What you read in the next chapter are his words. I will then return for the final chapters.

NOTES

1. Baiocchi and Ganuza, "Participatory Budgeting as If Emancipation Mattered."
2. Cabannes, "Participatory Budgeting."
3. Goldfrank, *Deepening Local Democracy in Latin America*.
4. Lerner and Schugurensky, "Who Learns What from Participating in Participatory Budgeting?"
5. Pateman, "Participatory Democracy Revisited."
6. Sintomer, Herzberg, and Röcke, "Participatory Budgeting in Europe."
7. Wampler, *Participatory Budgeting in Brazil*.
8. Sintomer, Herzberg, and Röcke, "Participatory Budgeting in Europe."

9. Cabannes, "Participatory Budgeting."
10. Baiocchi, *Militants and Citizens*.
11. Sintomer, Herzberg, and Röcke, "Participatory Budgeting in Europe."
12. Wampler, *Participatory Budgeting in Brazil*.
13. Baiocchi, *Militants and Citizens*.
14. Goldfrank, *Deepening Local Democracy in Latin America*.
15. Sintomer, Herzberg, and Röcke, "Participatory Budgeting in Europe."
16. Goldfrank, *Deepening Local Democracy in Latin America*.
17. Wampler, *Participatory Budgeting in Brazil*.
18. Sintomer, Herzberg, and Röcke, "Participatory Budgeting in Europe."
19. Lerner and Schugurensky, "Who Learns What from Participating in Participatory Budgeting."
20. Baiocchi and Ganuza, "Participatory Budgeting as If Emancipation Mattered."
21. Pateman, "Participatory Democracy Revisited."
22. Baiocchi and Ganuza, "Participatory Budgeting as If Emancipation Mattered."
23. Lerner and Secondo, "By the People, for the People."
24. Goldfrank, *Deepening Local Democracy in Latin America*.
25. Sintomer, Herzberg, and Röcke, "Participatory Budgeting in Europe."
26. Lerner and Schugurensky, "Who Learns What from Participating in Participatory Budgeting."
27. Dahl, *On Democracy*.
28. Fung and Wright, "Thinking about Empowered Participatory Governance."
29. Lerner and Secondo, "By the People, for the People."
30. Cabannes, "Participatory Budgeting."
31. Fung and Wright, "Thinking about Empowered Participatory Governance."
32. Touchton and Wampler, "Improving Social Well-Being through New Democratic Institutions."
33. Gonçalves, "The Effects of Participatory Budgeting on Municipal Expenditures and Infant Mortality in Brazil."
34. Fung and Wright, "Thinking about Empowered Participatory Governance."
35. Lerner and Secondo, "By the People, for the People."
36. Cabannes, "The Impact of Participatory Budgeting on Basic Services."
37. Fung, "Varieties of Participation in Complex Governance."
38. Cabannes, "The Impact of Participatory Budgeting on Basic Services."
39. Gilman, "Engaging Citizens."
40. Su, "Does Participation in Participatory Budgeting Improve the Legitimacy of Local Government?"
41. Moore, "Participatory Budgeting."
42. City of Vallejo, "Participatory Budgeting Vallejo."
43. PB NYC, "Participatory Budgeting in New York City."
44. City of Seattle, "Youth Voice, Youth Choice: Participatory Budgeting Results."
45. Gilman, "Engaging Citizens."
46. Phoenix Union High School District, "Participatory Budgeting."

47. Lander, "Participatory Budgeting in District 39."
48. New York City Council, "Participatory Budgeting: Cycle 4 Report."
49. City of Boston, "Youth Lead the Change: Participatory Budgeting Boston."

Chapter 7

Case Study

Victoria Independent School District

Many people may have preconceived perceptions of social justice and how to combat the issue. They may or may not be able to identify the possible root causes. In this chapter, we will investigate the use of participatory budgeting (PB) within the Victoria Independent School District (VISD) in multiple school settings as a means to empower marginalized communities and foster a more equitable distribution of resources. By engaging students, parents, and educators in the decision-making process, PB not only encourages active citizenship but also addresses the needs and priorities of those directly affected by social inequalities. Through this initiative, we will explore how this practical democratic approach to budgeting can contribute to dismantling systemic barriers and promoting social justice, ultimately leading to more inclusive and transformative educational experiences for all students.

Too often, people in administrative positions end up making decisions for what they perceive to be best for the organization. Why is this the case? It is not the name of the building or the brand that is represented; it is the people who make the organization what it is or what it has become. So, when it comes to making decisions about what to purchase or what programs/initiatives to start, why do we not allow the people in the organization to have a voice? With the use of PB, this allows stakeholders to use a voice that represents what the people want. As a result, it is not one person making decisions; rather, it is the collective voice. By using this democratic process in our school system, we foster a community-wide voice and allocate funds based on what the stakeholders deem best fit. No one person is above all others or is tasked with making all the decisions, and at the end of the project, majority rules. Of course, there are obvious guardrails that need to be set, but we can put a group of stakeholders together and come up with common ground as we roll out the project. Social justice/injustice is realized by allowing groups to have a voice.

A PRINCIPAL'S PERSPECTIVE ON BUDGETING

The process of school budgeting is often a conversation held between groups of people associated with the "business" of running a school: school board members, superintendents, and campus administration. Students and teachers usually do not see the nuts and bolts that happen behind the scenes of budgeting. They are on the receiving end of the budget—from salaries to copy paper, from books to paper clips, art supplies to sports equipment. The ones closest to the supply and demand of budgeting, staff, and students are often the least heard. At best, they rely on booster clubs, donations, or their own personal monies to bridge the gaps between student needs and what school allotments provide.

Embracing PB requires a shift in traditional decision-making processes and a willingness to relinquish some control. It takes courage to challenge the status quo and try new things, especially when it comes to allocating resources in a more inclusive and transparent manner. It requires placing faith in the collective wisdom of the school community, which can be a leap of faith for principals who are often entrenched in a traditional model of budgeting and allocation. Relying on the school community goes beyond the small nucleus of administrators who often make all decisions regarding money and resources.

However, while this is a daunting task, it is essential to recognize that stakeholder experiences and insights are invaluable in understanding the true needs of the school. By fostering a sense of ownership and agency in shaping the budget, principals foster a culture of collaboration and shared responsibility. PB enhances the decision-making process but also builds trust, strengthens relationships, and empowers individuals to become active change agents in the school community.

Implementing PB also requires a commitment to ongoing evaluation and reflection. When starting this process, know that there is no blanketed plan to fit the needs of every school in the rollout process. This is where your creative thinking skills will be challenged. As a principal, it is crucial to continuously assess the effectiveness and impact of this approach, adapting and refining it based on feedback and lessons learned.

This willingness to learn and adapt demonstrates a growth mindset and a genuine dedication to creating a more just and equitable educational environment. It takes courage to acknowledge when certain strategies may not be yielding the desired outcomes and to pivot toward alternative solutions. By fostering a culture of continuous improvement and learning, a principal can inspire innovation and create an atmosphere where experimentation and calculated risk-taking are celebrated.

DEMOGRAPHICS OF VICTORIA

Victoria is a city located in the southeastern part of Texas, and it is the seat of Victoria County. The city is known for its rich history, cultural diversity, and thriving economy. In relation to larger cities, Victoria is approximately a two-hour drive to San Antonio, Houston, and Corpus Christi. The city has a population of approximately sixty-eight thousand people, and it has experienced steady growth in recent years.

According to the US Census Bureau, Victoria's population is predominantly Hispanic or Latino, with nearly 54.9 percent followed by the next largest racial group of white consisting of 34.4 percent of the population. African Americans, Asian Americans, and other racial groups make up the remaining 10.7 percent of the population.

Victoria has a relatively young population, with a median age of 36.9 years. The largest age group in Victoria is individuals between the ages of twenty-five and forty-four, who make up nearly 30 percent of the population. Children younger than age eighteen make up approximately 26 percent of the population, indicating a significant need for quality education in the area. The education statistics in Victoria are impressive, with the city boasting a high percentage of residents who have completed some form of postsecondary education. Approximately 20 percent of residents hold a bachelor' degree or higher, while 82 percent have graduated from high school. The median household income in Victoria is $59,010, which is slightly lower than the national average.

When looking at the school districts in Victoria, there is just one public school district that serves the city and much of the surrounding county: VISD. VISD covers 612 square miles and is the largest district within Region 3, serving approximately fourteen thousand students across twenty-eight schools, including fourteen elementary schools, four middle schools, and two high schools. The district has a diverse student population, with approximately 67 percent Hispanic students, 24 percent white students, and 6 percent African American students.

The student population in VISD is relatively evenly distributed across grade levels, with approximately 33 percent of students in elementary school, 31 percent in middle school, and 36 percent in high school. The district has a student-to-teacher ratio of 15:1, which is slightly higher than the Texas state average of 14:1. Despite this, the district has a graduation rate of approximately 97 percent, which is significantly higher than the state average of 92 percent.

AT-RISK STUDENT DEMOGRAPHICS

The term *at risk* refers to students who face one or more factors that may make it more difficult for them to succeed in school. These factors can include low academic performance, poverty, limited English proficiency, or a history of absenteeism or discipline problems. Being identified as at risk can make a student eligible for additional support and resources to help them succeed in school. According to data from the Texas Education Agency, VISD has a significant number of students who are considered at risk of dropping out or failing to graduate on time. In the 2020–2021 school year, the district reported that 7,158 students, or 54 percent of the total student population, were considered at risk. We celebrate our graduation rate, as it belies the expectations of students at risk of not graduating.

Within VISD, the largest group of at-risk students are those who are economically disadvantaged, with 9,119 students, or 68.8 percent of the total student population, falling into this category. Additionally, 964 students, or 7.3 percent, are considered at risk due to limited English proficiency, and 1,694 students, or 8 percent, have been identified as having a disability that may impact their academic success.

The district has implemented a range of programs and initiatives aimed at supporting at-risk students and improving their academic outcomes. For example, the district's Early College program allows eligible high school students to earn college credit while still in high school, helping them get a head start on their postsecondary education. All or nearly all of their tuition costs are covered either by the district or VISD Education Foundation. In recent years, we have worked to make more dual-credit courses available within the high schools by deploying P-TECH schools, thereby eliminating the barrier of access that is transportation to and from the college. The district also offers a variety of specialized programs, such as bilingual and special education services, to support students with diverse learning needs.

Overall, while the number of at-risk students in VISD is significant, the district is working to provide these students with the resources and support they need to succeed in school and beyond. We are experiencing great success. By continuing to prioritize the needs of at-risk students, VISD can help ensure that all students can achieve academic success and reach their full potential.

Case Study

PB ROLLOUT AT VISD

Our superintendent of schools, Dr. Quintin Shepherd, introduced the idea and process of PB with the comment, "The people most impacted by our decisions should have the greatest voice in those decisions." In July 2022, he met with me, high school principal Justin Gabrysch, and then posed the question, "What would you do to improve student learning with $100,000?" Intrigued by the idea, we asked the same question to the leadership team at East High School. In a subsequent conversation shortly thereafter, we discussed my potential role in helping lead the initiative if we chose to scale this throughout the district. VISD makes a concerted effort to differentiate between mentoring experiences and sponsoring experiences. This is part of our culture and systemic architecture around leadership development at all levels. Often, administrators (and teachers) are sponsored into leadership roles, which comes with it all the benefits of mentoring, but also real power in the form of decision-making.

Over the course of two weeks, we agreed that I would be leading the initiative not just at our high school but also supporting the work happening at other campuses throughout the district including Victoria West High School and our four middle schools (Harold Cade, Patti Welder, Stroman/STEM academy, and Howell). Support from the district office would come from the superintendent, deputy superintendent, and other departments as needed. The overarching vision was that students and staff in VISD would brainstorm, evaluate, and prioritize needs to come up with a ballot to give their peers a choice in what programs they wanted to close learning gaps. In the end, students would vote to determine how the monies should be allocated, and teachers would write grants to apply for programs they thought would align with student needs.

In fall 2022, an overview rollout plan was decided and described: Along with the leadership team, we met with Victoria East High School stakeholders (teachers and students) to discuss a vision of the best ways to spend the money. Once those discussions were finalized, the entire student body, faculty, and staff would vote as to how the money would be spent. We decided that in November, just a week after the nation voted, students and faculty would line the hallways to cast their ballots to determine how the money would be spent.

In the ensuing weeks, various ways to roll out the PB plan were discussed, including how to incorporate other campuses into the process. Every campus is unique and has different needs, and the ideals of PB would allow each school to determine how best to roll out their own process. Although it might look slightly different at each campus, we would remain true to the process and concept of PB. School principals at all campuses were enthusiastic about the potential benefits of improving student learning.

THE IMPORTANCE OF TARGETS, METRICS, AND GOALS

Before the rollout of using PB in a school, it is important to establish clear targets, metrics, and goals to guide the implementation process and measure its effectiveness. Think of this as quality assurance. As you consider the process, be sure to think about the big picture and the overall outcomes you hope to achieve. This involves envisioning a school community where students feel empowered, staff have a sense of ownership, and where resource allocation reflects the diverse needs and priorities of all stakeholders. By setting ambitious yet attainable targets and metrics, you can ensure that PB serves as a catalyst for transformative change.

We understood there were certain aspects we needed to consider such as ensuring the greatest amount of participation, setting limits on the dollar amounts, and making sure a diverse group of students from a wide spectrum of cultural backgrounds, socioeconomic status, and grade levels were represented.

In our conversations, we all understood that having participation was a top priority. We wanted to set targets for participation rates among the various stakeholders, including students and teachers. Measuring the level of engagement and involvement through a ThoughtExchange, the number of proposals submitted and the number of votes cast would help ensure not only diversity but also equity.

Regarding budget allocation, each school would be responsible for monitoring the distribution of funds across various areas, such as educational resources and student support services. We knew that tracking these expenditures would be crucial to measure the extent to which the funds associated aligned with the identified needs and priorities of the school community, ensuring that resources were directed in a manner that helped close learning gaps. It was also imperative to track the use of funds for federal accounting related to the funding stream.

Our discussions were focused on establishing our priority to drive educational outcomes, foster a sense of community, and promote the democratic values of active citizenship. It soon became apparent that measuring the impact on student learning would impact the school climate and the overall educational experience of students. It is important to note that targets, metrics, and goals may vary depending on the specific context and priorities of the school. Regular evaluation and feedback loops should be established to assess progress, identify areas for improvement, and refine the participatory budgeting process over time.

THE PUBLIC LAUNCH OF PB AT VISD

In August, East High School leadership first presented the plan to the Guiding Coalition, a group of teachers who head the departments on campus, as well as a group of forty student leaders from various organizations on the East campus to gather a wide array of viewpoints and ideas. Once again, the question was asked, "What would you do with "$100,000?" Together, they created and ran a "ThoughtExchange." This process activates and elevates student voice through crowdsourcing software to get feedback on students' wants and needs. Students were told they could submit as many ideas as they wanted as long as their ideas supported "improving student learning" or "eliminating learning gaps." Students then became ambassadors for change among their peers to encourage students to participate in posting their ideas on ThoughtExchange.

The ThoughtExchange was coupled with an informational video to kick-start the process of generating school needs from the student body. The middle schools also followed suit. The ideas shared were astounding! Student ideas ranged from providing "real-world experiences," to accessing more mental health resources. Students also mentioned better access to technology and tutoring to assist them in college and career preparation. In a further expansion on social justice, the school team ensured that access to participation within the ThoughtExchange process was not a barrier by offering access to technology during the school day.

Some students shared their ideas via technology using cell phones or school technology. Some students worked with a teacher or peer "buddy" to ensure that each voice was heard. Students for whom English is not their first language watched videos with their teachers and participated giving immediate feedback, as well.

Once the ThoughtExchange closed, the assistant principals worked with the Guiding Coalition to identify students from a wide spectrum of student groups to help sift through the thousands of ideas generated. This group of students came from every grade level and represented a diversity of academic, ethnic, and economic backgrounds. The plan was for the students to meet weekly with administration and the Guiding Coalition to discuss the students' wants and needs expressed in the ThoughtExchange. The work of the Guiding Coalition and the student group was to distill the ideas generated into a cohesive ballot so that the student body could then vote.

When it came time to vote, all history classes were given a day to report to the voting booths set up around the campus. Each student was given a pencil paper ballot along with the description of each proposal. Students who were enrolled in dual-credit courses were called down during an elective class and given the same opportunity. Students and staff both had the opportunity to vote and more than two thousand ballots were cast. This was democracy in action and on campus.

The numbers were decided based on the grouping of topics through the Exchange. For example, Real World and Career Readiness received the most proposals. Therefore, the steering committee decided to allocate the most funds for these two topics. Technology and Mental Health received the next highest interest and as such, slightly less dollars were available.

While implementing this process, students and staff gained a greater sense of connection and belonging in the school system. Students took the opportunity to visit with peers, teachers, and parents about the happenings within the school and gained a greater sense of ownership in how the school functions daily.

Not only were students and teachers able to come together for the greater good but it also opened their eyes and made them realize others have different

TEXTBOX 7.1
SAMPLE HIGH SCHOOL BALLOT:

Ballot 1: Real World and College and Career Readiness:

- A. Real World - $50,000
  College and Career Readiness - $30,000
- B. Real World - $40,000
  College and Career Readiness - $40,000
- C. Real World - $30,000
  College and Career Readiness - $50,000

Ballot 2: Technology and Mental Health

- A. Technology - $18,000
  Mental Health - $2,000
- B. Technology - $15,000
  Mental Health - $5,000
- C. Technology - $12,000
  Mental Health - $8,000

needs than their own. Student leaders had their own *aha* moments when they discovered that their peers often did not have the same opportunities as they did.

Students and staff worked together in small groups and had conversations around different viewpoints and possible middle ground where all could agree. Through these conversations, it became evident that both teachers and students were able to build relationships not only with the steering committee members but also stakeholders within the school. Students and staff were able to use their voices and see the impact of coming around a table to have conversations while keeping an open mind. This is a core element of leadership development. As students gained new insights and ways of seeing the world, their minds opened up.

Once the ballots were counted, it was time for students and teachers to submit proposals for review (an example can be found at the end of this chapter). Teachers and students met to review the funding proposals and to provide feedback on the feasibility and impact of each proposal.

During the review process, teachers and students looked at each project proposal and evaluated it for its potential impact, feasibility, and reasonableness. After this initial review, the group discussed and debated the proposals, providing more feedback and recommendations. This group discussion was critical to ensure that all perspectives were taken into account and that all decisions were made collaboratively.

Once all the proposals had been reviewed and discussed, the student leaders and teacher leaders took a silent vote and provided their recommendations to the school administration. The school administration then funded the proposals based on the recommendations. This was made more challenging due to the demands of after-school commitments that demanded teacher and student time. The committee soon learned that students were more than capable of finding suitable replacements. The same was true for faculty and staff. For this reason, it was crucial to review the process and criteria at the beginning of every meeting. A willingness to be flexible only increased stakeholder participation and ownership, which in turn, creates a bigger democratic impact.

Students and staff in the school community were asked how the process made them feel, what they thought the next steps should be, and what they looked forward to. When visiting with students, we realized a shift in the mindset during our discussions. Students began to realize that not all of their peers have the same opportunities to experience life after high school. Conversations started to change when students shared their stories about wanting to go to college, but families had to work on limited incomes, even if they just wanted to visit. Soon all students began to realize that certain projects would mean more to their classmates. Teacher Johnathan Sixtos shared a similar sentiment, "I love to see students participate in the budget process. Since everyone gets to vote, it ensures equity across all populations and empowers them to make meaningful decisions that directly impact their education! Now, the kids get to see how their voices and choices change our school for the better."

Students also shared perceptions of belonging and advocacy. Izabela wisely stated, "It was eye-opening to give opportunities to people who don't normally get them, who wouldn't normally envision these experiences for themselves." Jack agreed, "It was an epiphany of real-world experiences that normally a lot of kids wouldn't get." The heartfelt discussions changed the viewpoints of several in the room and the topic of equity was on the minds of many. The Victoria East team noted a key takeaway from this process: perceptions of increased stakeholder ownership. Because the community members identified their own needs, the process felt different from experiences in which mandates came from a distant entity that had little to no connection to the people it should be helping.

After months of hard work, our school community began to reap the benefits of the accepted proposals that received funding through this process. For example, one group used the advantage of PB to fund college visits across the region. These visits provided students with an opportunity to explore potential colleges and universities and get a taste of what college life is like. This may not seem like much, but for a community that is largely at risk, this is pivotal.

Other groups used PB to fund a book study program focused on reducing anxiety and promoting calmness. Participants in the program met once a week in a "Calm My Thoughts" group to read and discuss strategies to manage stress and anxiety.

Another chose to fund an initiative to promote cultural understanding and awareness. For instance, this group chose to fund and organize a religion and culture field trip, which took students to different religious houses and cultural sites in the community, giving students a chance to learn more about the beliefs and practices of different cultures.

Last, one large group consisting of the Fine Arts and Athletics programs rallied together to create an initiative to support youth leadership development. Funds were allocated to create leadership camps for students to develop communication, problem-solving, and decision-making skills—tools necessary for success in any field.

All of these opportunities provided students with the ability to network with peers who share interests and goals, creating a supportive community to help them achieve their aspirations.

PERSONAL REFLECTION

Personally, this process has allowed me to visit with staff and students and really try to get a pulse on what our teachers and students feel they need to be successful. During our time together rolling out this process, our conversations allowed me to see aspects of the school from a different vantage point. Imagine the balcony over a dance floor. By standing on the balcony, you can see groups of people engaging in conversations and maybe certain groups start to form. You see body language used in conversations, but you cannot always hear the conversation. Now, go walk on the dance floor and listen to the conversations. Your perspective changes! You are able to listen to what others are saying; you can engage in the discussion and now have open two-way communication. This process has allowed me to engage in conversations and feel connected to our students and staff. From looking at things through a different lens, my perspective changed. Also, while I myself have learned, our students and staff have learned from one another. Often students only see the small world around them and are unable to see the big picture. Through conversations, our students gained a respect for their classmates who might not have the same opportunities as they have. The small things that we often overlook are now coming into view.

I remember one conversation that came up while visiting with our students during the process. Several of our students did not realize that other peers did not have the same upbringing. The students were unaware that some of their peers had never left Victoria or had never stepped foot on a college campus. Soon through our conversation, they realized that college campus visits, trade school visits, and field trips might be more important than their own desire, needs, or wants. This conversation allowed our students to walk in someone else's shoes just for a moment. During that realization, their perspective changed and the compassion for others came to light.

VICTORIA EAST HIGH SCHOOL

Participatory Budgeting Proposal
2022–2023 Guidelines

- Purpose: The Participatory Budgeting program is designed to encourage, facilitate, recognize, and award funding to innovative and inspirational proposals that improve student learning and/or bridge the learning gap.
- Persons Eligible to Apply for Grants: Individuals employed by the Victoria Independent School District and VEHS students may apply. All applications must be sponsored by a VEHS staff member.

- Eligible Proposals: Proposal designed to take place by June 30, 2023, school year that meet the selection criteria noted below are eligible for consideration.
- Award of Funds: Grants will be awarded through four funding categories. Awards will continue until the funds are depleted or until the deadline whichever comes first. Funding categories include:

  1. Real-World Experiences that will improve student learning (as defined on attachment A);
  2. College and Career Readiness that will improve student learning (as defined on attachment A);
  3. Technology that will improve student learning (as defined on attachment A);
  4. Mental Health projects that will improve student learning (as defined on attachment A).

Proposal Application Release Date: January 16, 2023
Proposal Application Deadline: April 28, 2023
Selection Criteria: The following items will be considered during the proposal review process:

1. The degree to which the proposal addresses improved student learning and/or closing the learning gap.
2. The degree to which the proposal represents a creative or innovative approach to the accomplishment of improved student learning and/or closing the learning gap.
3. The degree to which sound evaluation procedures are incorporated in the proposal.
4. The degree to which the proposal is clear and logical, including:
   a. A compelling needs statement;
   b. Clearly stated objectives;
   c. Clear descriptions of instructional procedures, methods of treatments; and
   d. Clearly explain the connection between needs, objectives, and evaluation procedures.

Selection Process

1. The deadline for all proposals is 3:00 p.m. on April 28, 2023.
   a. Proposal applications must be fully complete and signed by the sponsor(s).

2. Applications will be reviewed and by the Participatory Budgeting Committee comprised of the VEHS's Guiding Coalition, selected Student Leaders, and select admin members. The majority vote will determine the proposal's status, and all voting will be done with silent ballots.
3. The review process will be held every two weeks until funds run out, or the application deadline is reached.
4. For each proposal application submitted, the Participatory Budgeting Committee shall make one of the following determinations:
   a. Approved
   b. Approved with pending conditions and/or modifications
   c. Disapproved
5. Applicants will be notified of decisions within one week of the review meeting.
6. Projects must be implemented before the June 30 deadline.

Responsibilities of Participatory Budgeting Proposal Recipients:

1. Use the awards for the purposes intended.
2. Implement and evaluate projects within one month of the completed project.
3. Prepare a Final Report. The Final Report template is attached.
4. Share information about successful projects in staff development sessions, if requested.
5. Share photos and/or videos of the project of students, if requested.

Responsibilities Committee member:

1. Ensure the applicant has filed the Final Report by the due date.
2. Ensure the review process is completed with integrity.

Guidelines for Completing the Application

1. A project is appropriate if "yes" can be answered to the following questions:
   Is there a need?
   - Is the project innovative and/or creative?
   - Will it improve student learning/understanding?
   - Can it be done?
   - Is it practical?
2. Suggestions for strong applications

Do's
- Proof the application for spelling, grammar, and punctuation.
- Be realistic. Make sure that what you are asking for can be achieved.
- Be specific and thorough.
- Complete all items on the application.
- Include measurable outcomes

Don'ts
- Don't be vague or submit incomplete responses.
- Don't give up if your proposal is not approved. Keep trying!

3. Critical Elements of the Application Form

Budget
- Itemize expenses and round to the nearest dollar.
- Include the VISD budget code, vendor name, purchase quantities and amounts. New vendors (new technologies and services) not included on the VISD vendor list *are* allowed; however, supplies that can be purchased from VISD-approved vendors *must* be utilized. The approved vendor list is located at https://www.visd.net/, then click on the Menu tab, then scroll down and click on Central Supply and Purchasing, and then click on the VISD Approved Vendor List.
- Avoid requests for salaries and stipends, as they will not be funded. However, extra duty pay may be requested for noncontract hours.
- Explain the costs associated with the project.

Statement of Need
- Explain what the need is in detail.
- Give data to support the need.

Statement of Purpose
- Tell how you hope to achieve improved learning.
- Keep the statement straightforward.
- Promise only that which you can reasonably expect to achieve.

Statement of Learning Outcomes
- Demonstrate that the project will improve learning outcomes more than existing practices do.
- Explain the type of learning the project will support.

Methods and Procedures
- Describe instructional procedures (including timelines), methods, or activities that will be utilized.
- Relate methods and procedures to Purpose and Learning Outcomes.

Evaluation Design
- State how results will be measured.
- Explain how evaluation data are related to the stated objectives.
- Project how many students will be impacted.

- Explain how you will know whether the project was successful.

School/Community Partners
- Identify school/community partners, if any, involved in the project and their respective roles.

4. Submission of Application
   a. The deadline for submission of all application material is 3:00 p.m. April 28, 2023.
   b. All required application material must be submitted to one of the AP secretaries, Ms. Zarboch, or Mrs. Trujillio.
5. Inquiries may be directed to Suzann Creager.

Grant Application Evaluation Process:

Budget:
1. Is the itemized budget information clear and complete?
2. Is the budget narrative appropriate and necessary to complete the proposal's plan?

Need:
1. Is the need clearly stated, and does it provide data to support the need?

Purpose:
1. Is the purpose clearly stated, and does it include intended innovative or inspirational student outcomes?

Learning Outcomes:
1. Does it clearly state measurable student learning outcomes?
2. Does it relate student learning outcomes?

Methods and Procedures:
1. Are procedures, methods, activities, and timelines specifically stated?
2. Are activities/procedures directly related to Learning Outcomes?

Evaluation Design:
1. Does the Evaluation Design (including timelines for data collection) clearly describe how it will measure the success of the project?
2. Does it clearly align evaluation measures with project Learning Outcomes?

Chapter 8

Final Thoughts for Superintendents

In the previous chapter, you received a detailed and comprehensive explanation of a massive and systemic participatory budgeting (PB) project that occurred in Victoria, Texas. As superintendent of the district, I was thrilled to see this project evolve under Principal Gabrysch's leadership. It was further moving to see and hear how much our students and teachers embraced the process.

In the majority of university leadership programs across the United States, a foundational course on leadership is typically incorporated early in the curriculum. Within these courses, students are exposed to various leadership theories and actively participate in thought-provoking and intellectually stimulating discussions. A recurring theme in these dialogues is the binary classification of leadership as either "good" or "bad." As a professor who has taught at diverse institutions in three different states over the past two decades, I can attest to this tendency during the course to categorize and evaluate leadership. It is an intrinsic human inclination to assess and form judgments about various aspects of life, including leadership. Numerous individuals can easily identify leaders they perceive as good or bad and provide rationales for their assessments. This topic will be examined in more detail later in this chapter; however, it is worthwhile to pose the following questions at this juncture: Was the PB project beneficial for Victoria Independent School District (VISD) community? Does this instance exemplify good leadership, and if so, why?

To engage in a more comprehensive analysis of these questions, it is vital to consider several factors that may contribute to the determination of effective or ineffective leadership. Factors such as the ethical foundation, decision-making processes, communication skills, and the ability to adapt and respond to unforeseen challenges should be taken into account when evaluating the quality of leadership. Furthermore, it is essential to recognize that leadership is not a monolithic concept, and what may be deemed as effective or successful leadership in one context may not necessarily be applicable to another.

In the context of the PB project and the VISD community, a thorough examination of the various dimensions of leadership can offer valuable insights into the effectiveness of the initiative and the leadership qualities displayed. By analyzing the ethical principles guiding the project, the decision-making strategies employed, the channels of communication between the leaders and the community, and the ability of the leadership to adapt to the evolving needs of the community, a more nuanced understanding of the leadership in this particular situation can be attained.

Ultimately, the determination of whether the PB project constitutes good leadership is a subjective assessment that may vary depending on the individual's perspective and the criteria they consider most significant. Nevertheless, engaging in a scholarly and professional exploration of the topic and considering the multifaceted nature of leadership can provide a deeper understanding of the complexities involved in evaluating leadership and facilitate more informed judgments on the matter.

In this chapter, we will briefly revisit the PB project from VISD in the context of a theory of action. We will explore it as a series of if-then statements that build on one another. We will see how each step made the next one possible and why. We will examine the role of the superintendent in this process, paying special attention to the role of the superintendent as it relates to either the scope of the project or size of the district. We will also reframe PB as a thinking framework and provide some thoughts about how a superintendent might use this framework to identify gaps in the transformational structures being built in the district. Next will be a brief exploration into seeing the bigger picture and how to apply this framework to your daily thinking. Finally, we will revisit goals and purposes and end with a brief discussion of leadership in an endeavor to answer these questions.

WHERE DID THE PROJECT REALLY START?

The disbursement of the Elementary and Secondary School Emergency Relief (ESSER) funds over the period from 2020 to 2024 has been a crucial element in addressing the educational challenges brought on by the COVID-19 pandemic. Throughout these years, educational institutions have implemented various strategies and initiatives with the objective of enhancing student learning and mitigating achievement gaps. Consequently, an opportunity has emerged to assess the effectiveness of these strategies and explore innovative approaches for utilizing any remaining funds.

ESSER funding has been disbursed in three major rounds, beginning with the Coronavirus Aid, Relief, and Economic Security (CARES) Act in March 2020, followed by the Coronavirus Response and Relief Supplemental Appropriations (CRRSA) Act in December 2020, and finally, the American Rescue Plan (ARP) Act in March 2021. These funding packages have provided substantial financial resources to support schools in their efforts to adapt to the pandemic and continue offering quality education.

In the upcoming decade, extensive research will be conducted from federal, state, and university perspectives to analyze the effectiveness of the various strategies employed during this period. The team at VISD has expressed a keen interest in evaluating the effectiveness of these initiatives from the onset of the funding. This interest stems from their commitment to quality assurance and effective resource management in all aspects of their educational endeavors.

By adopting a scholarly and professional approach, VISD aims to contribute valuable insights to the broader educational community and promote data-driven decision-making in the allocation and utilization of ESSER funds. This comprehensive analysis will ultimately enhance our understanding of the most effective strategies for mitigating the adverse effects of the COVID-19 pandemic on student learning and achievement.

The genesis of Victoria's PB project came as a result of a thought experiment regarding the allocation of remaining ESSER funds in K–12 education. It was nearly assured that every district would likely overbudget and underspend ESSER funds, and VISD leadership wanted to create an effective spend-down plan for any of those remaining funds. VISD elected to go with PB. With divergent priorities among stakeholders, it was recognized that PB could create a more democratic and equitable process for decision-making and help further its development as a transformational school district. VISD recognized that by embracing this collaborative approach, schools could foster a sense of ownership and commitment to the chosen projects, promoting successful implementation and lasting positive impact. VISD further believed this project would advance a belief around building a strong supportive systemic structure to support transformational change, the tenants of the framework described throughout this book.

THEORY OF ACTION: IF-THEN

If a superintendent could estimate the remaining ESSER funding available (e.g., 5 percent), then they have a funding target. If that superintendent uses the theory of action described in this book, they consider how to flow these funds in a way that creates a deep equity in the use of those funds. PB is certainly not the only way this could occur. The key to equity is recognition that equity is all about access. Who has access to what resources and supports? Who has access to what information? Equitable access means radical transparency and allowing full access to the people who will be most impacted by the decision.

For instance, purchasing an online tutoring program may (or may not) be an equitable use of funding. In VISD, many students do not have access to internet from their homes, and parents/caregivers are reluctant to use mobile hotspots. Further, parental support in using technology in the home is limited. Providing hotspots, laptops, and online tutoring creates an equity divide in a district like VISD because students who have support get more support and students with low or no support cannot access additional supports. VISD knows this to be true because they kept track of key usage metrics throughout the pandemic.

VISD was deliberate about authentic equity with this funding. It was important that whatever use the funding would ultimately be put to would have the maximum level of student voice and maximum level of equity of access, which is the strongest path to equality of outcome. If a district committed to spending these funds on a PB project (of any scale), then the district could have a conversation about quality assurance.

Quality assurance within the context of PB is a matter of asking several initial questions at the outset. What do we hope to accomplish? When do these funds need to be incumbered and spent? How will we know if these projects are effective? What level of impact do we hope to achieve? Who will be appointed to manage the project? What supports will this person have? Do we have a PB framework to follow (VISD did not but found one quickly as described in the previous two chapters)? A small cadre of district office administrators worked through these questions, and quickly we decided to involve Principal Gabrysch as project manager. Once the rudimentary quality assurance pieces were in place, then VISD could begin the conversation around ownership.

As described in the previous chapter, there were several paths to ownership. First, ownership was sought from the other campus principals who would be running these projects on their campuses. Next came ownership from the teachers who would be part of this process over the course of several months as it developed. The goal was for as much student ownership as possible, which meant creating steering committees and supporting these students in every step during the process. Ownership can only work if administration is humble enough to approach people with problems and not always with solutions. PB was not a solution so much as it was a problem to solve. How could this be structured in such a way to get maximum student involvement? This driving question garnered deep ownership from the various communities. The priorities of administrators, teachers, and students often diverge when it comes to allocating resources for improving student learning. PB offered a solution to this disconnect by involving all relevant stakeholders in the decision-making process. This approach is based on the principles of democracy and seeks to ensure that those most affected by decisions have the greatest say in the outcome.

If there was deep ownership, then VISD could foster courageous leadership and policymaking. When the VISD students were asked to present at the statewide "Governance Camp" for the Texas Association of School Boards (TASB) at the conclusion of the PB project, VISD had moved into courageous leadership and policymaking. Trustees from VISD accompanied the students to the camp to help support and answer governance-related questions. Later in that same year, VISD was asked to present at the TASB Summer Leadership Institute for all trustees throughout the state of Texas. The VISD PB project had grown from a micro impact at the campus level, through an impact at the district level, to an impact at the state level, which culminated with a macro impact at the national level in two ways. The first was an article published in *School Administrator* by AASA[1] related to the VISD PB project. The second was when Principal Gabrysch was asked to participate as part of a panel on creative financing through ESSER as part of a national conference and forum.

If this courageous leadership and policymaking are in place, then we can begin cultivating public will and understanding for transformation, which is ongoing. This book hopefully has you thinking about PB and, more importantly, about this theory of action. And if you are thinking about it, then the theory of action has worked because together we are cultivating public will and understanding for transformation. My charge to you is to pass this knowledge on to someone else (or even better, encourage them to buy the book!).

Remember, a theory of action is forward-thinking and exists as a series of if-then statements. The framework described throughout this book exists as a planning tool in this regard. PB as launched and described at VISD was a theory of action to reinforce the supportive systemic structures that allow for transformation within schools. Also remember, though, this theory of action can be used as a backward-thinking framework. This can be very helpful when you find yourself in the middle of a project and things are going wrong.

THINKING FRAMEWORK

Utilizing this analytical framework necessitates the ability to engage in nonjudgmental critical analysis when reflecting on past experiences. Achieving this level of impartiality is a challenging endeavor, often requiring years of practice to master. A rigorous critical analysis of any project is essential for growth and learning. However, when judgment becomes intertwined with this analysis, it often leads to the formation of excuses, which impede progress and inhibit learning. Conversely, explanations serve to bring us closer to our objectives.

To overcome this challenge, consider employing the following technique: Reflect on a project or task that did not meet expectations within the past few weeks or months. Narrate the events and the factors that contributed to the unfavorable outcome in your mind. Now, take a moment to vocalize this narrative, recounting the events aloud. Finally, recount the story once more, this time assuming full responsibility for the outcome (you cannot blame anyone else).

Upon comparison, it is likely that the initial account contained a considerable degree of judgment, while the subsequent retelling was largely devoid of such biases. Admittedly, the latter narrative may be more difficult to articulate, yet it is instrumental in fostering a more objective and constructive approach to critical analysis. By adopting this technique, you can enhance your ability to analyze past experiences impartially, ultimately facilitating growth and learning.

To be clear, by nearly any measure, our project was a success. Looking back on the PB project at VISD, however, there are many places we could improve our processes. Let us look at a few examples from different places in the framework to understand more deeply. We will look at equitable funding as a place for improvement, quality assurance, and ownership. Of course, VISD can find places for improvement at each of the stages because that is what learning organizations do. These examples are provided as illustrative cases.

Equitable funding stands as a remaining question. Equity of opportunity is the shortest path to equality of outcome. If equity of opportunity was important in this project, we must ask what opportunity existed for all students. The student steering committee was made up of students who were interested in the project, willing to dedicate some time outside of class to help manage the project, and able to be available to lead. Because the steering committee had some direction of the overall project, there is opportunity to make sure every student can access the opportunity to be on the steering committee. Equitable funding also relates to which projects got funded. Because this is a political process, there was campaigning. Successful campaigns often have more resources (not just money, but time, connections, and experience) than unsuccessful campaigns. VISD may wonder how many unsuccessful campaigns may have represented a more diverse population. This is a great opportunity for growth and learning.

Quality assurance was a strong component of project thinking, and like everything else, it can always be improved. In retrospect, laying out a goal for the steering committee to articulate the quality assurance guidelines for both the submissions and voting process may have been helpful and should be considered in future endeavors.

For ownership, the transition of idea from superintendent to a small task force of cabinet members was strong. That transition to Principal Gabrysch was strong. The transition from Principal Gabrysch to the other participating principals was not as strong. This is not the fault of any of the principals or executive cabinet. When I tell the story, I am the only one responsible. If I were to have a do-over, I would have spent more time after passing the PB project off to the project manager in meeting with the other principals directly to help answer questions, explain the rationale, and paint a bigger picture of what the project intended to do.

As difficult as this was to write for me (and share in this way), it gives evidence of a disciplined commitment to continuous improvement, which is part of the culture of VISD. This level of disciplined commitment is something you must have if you intend to use this tool as a thinking framework. With this in mind, I hope you will feel comfortable thinking about the last year of your leadership and asking, what could have gone better? Tell the story again as if you were the only one responsible. Find where that fits on the framework of this book. Start thinking. This is the path to improvement.

SEE THE BIGGER PICTURE

You never forget the first time you walk into the Amazon rainforest. Floating down the Amazon River, you have a sense of narrowing. The first time, everything is new. You become acutely aware that you are getting smaller and smaller, and as a result, even your field of vision narrows. Stepping off the boat, it is impossible to see the jungle even though the jungle is all around you. You focus on the people right in front of you, the path just beneath you, or the tree right before you. This was my experience and the experience of others I have met who have had a chance to visit the Amazon or some other remote locations. I did not actually see the whole rainforest until dinnertime. Evening came with a gathering in a space the village used for communal events and meals and preparing piranha for dinner. I had been hydrating dutifully throughout the day but sweating profusely. Finally, my bladder caught up with the water and I needed to step away. It was not until I was walking back into the community space that my vision opened up. I was no longer focused on the piranha, my bladder, or the fear that I would be attacked by a leopard. I saw a group of people huddled together around the fish. I saw a small group of children playing some version of stickball, which reminded me of home. I saw this small village surrounded by jungle rainforest. And I saw myself as part of that bigger picture. Different authors talk about seeing the picture in different ways. I will forever carry this image of the rainforest with me, and I think of it as "step back and reframe." Once I stepped back from the immediate and urgent and detached from the moment, I could see things I had never seen before. As a leadership skill, the step back and reframe move is a necessary ability and will save both you and your team hours upon hours of frustration. The ability to use frameworks requires you to step back, detach, and frame (and reframe).

The successful application of any thinking framework requires you to see your own decisions and actions with purposeful strange-making eyes. You must make strange your way of thinking and ask, why did I do it this way? What was I thinking? What wasn't I thinking? What if we are wrong? Poor superintendents use frameworks to justify bad decisions or weak thinking. Worse, they use frameworks to blame and shame others. How easy it would be to find flaws in a project and have a framework at hand and then find someone responsible who has dropped the ball, so to speak. Excellent superintendents use frameworks to hone their thinking skills to stay on a path of continuous improvement. Think for a moment about a project happening right now in your district. Think of a project where something has either gone wrong or just isn't happening the way you had initially planned. Stay in the moment and think about where things seem to be going wrong and ask yourself why. Now, step back. Consider the five-part framework and ask where these problems exist in the framework. Look now at the antecedent steps; did you complete those effectively? If not, you may have a foundation of sand. Regardless of where you focus, you now have a reframed approach you can share with your team. Step back to detach and reframe and then step back in to reengage.

Beyond step back and reframe, another way we often talk about this in education (especially with board members) is to think about the difference between the dance floor and balcony. The job of the superintendent is to run a lot of stairs! You will find yourself on the dance floor a lot. You have an obligation to run those stairs up to the balcony and share that information with your board. Their job is not to run stairs. That is your job. The step back and reframe is a balcony move. The easiest way to know if you are on the dance floor or the balcony is to think about seeing and listening. You listen from the dance floor. You see from the balcony. If you are spending a lot of time in meetings, planning meetings, design meetings, implementation meetings, accountability meetings, and so on, you are doing a lot of listening. Your view is likely myopic. It may be detailed but will be myopic. From the balcony, you see. Which groups are working together and which aren't? Who is not on the floor that should be? Are the dancers following the steps in the same way?

To do this you may need to be part of the conversation but not necessarily *in* the conversation.

There are many competencies for learning to lead, and one of them is to attempt to see everything through a lens of leadership. This is simply not possible if you are too close to the action. As superintendents, we are all guilty of designing plans and helping to implement those plans. This is the transformative work that is happening in all our schools every day. If we don't take the time to run up to the balcony, however, we are disabusing ourselves of the greatest resource imaginable, which is those board members who want to serve at their highest capacity as governance leaders. We simply need to run the stairs and share what is happening. Our job is to have myriad frameworks to help explain the action. The framework detailed in this book is a blueprint for how a board and superintendent support the transformational work happening on the dance floor.

You can start tomorrow. What is something you can commit to that is so small you cannot fail? Perhaps you can commit to having this conversation with your cabinet. For some, this might be something you can do. For others, this might be too much. I would suggest the smallest thing you could do if you desire to implement this thinking would be to simply put a copy of the graphic from chapter 5 (p. 96) on your desk. No further action is required; merely allow it to reside there, capturing your attention occasionally. When it does, you will be prompted to engage in reflection (stepping back) and contemplation (detachment). It is imperative to exercise discipline in mastering this framework, coupled with the fortitude to explore and acquire additional frameworks. These intellectual structures are abundant for those willing to seek them out. Frameworks serve as the crucial foundation enabling the transition from the dance floor to the balcony.

WHAT IS THE GOAL/PURPOSE?

Projects within educational districts must be designed to further district objectives and aspirations. Failure to align these initiatives with established priorities risks precipitating mission drift, which can have deleterious consequences. Such drift may manifest as confusion, diminished long-term support, frustration, apprehension, and anxiety among stakeholders.

Mission drift can arise from a lack of strategic alignment or an excessive number of initiatives that dilute organizational focus. The ensuing consequences include a decline in stakeholder engagement, suboptimal resource allocation, and diminished organizational effectiveness. By rigorously maintaining alignment between projects and district priorities, educational institutions can mitigate the risk of mission drift and foster an environment conducive to achieving their strategic goals.

When PB was initially introduced as a topic at the executive cabinet level, the discourse focused on discerning alignment opportunities with existing district priorities. This strategic approach ensured that PB did not materialize as an extraneous addition, but rather as an opportunity to bolster the advancement of objectives delineated within the VISD strategic plan.

As you have learned, PB is a powerful approach to allocating remaining ESSER funds in a democratic and inclusive manner. By involving all stakeholders in the decision-making process, schools can foster a sense of ownership and commitment to the chosen projects, promoting successful implementation and lasting positive impact. Furthermore, PB serves as an opportunity to teach students about democratic principles and civic engagement, helping to create a more informed and active citizenry. This advances the core purpose of education. According to John Dewey, the purpose of education is not the communication of knowledge but the sharing of social experience so that children become integrated into the democratic community.

A TEACHING OPPORTUNITY AND A POWERFUL MESSAGE

John Dewey (1859–1952) was a pioneering American philosopher and educator who significantly influenced the development of progressive education.[2] He believed that education should be an active, experiential process, wherein students engage with their environment and learn through inquiry and problem-solving.[3] Dewey argued that a focus on students' interests and needs, along with fostering cooperation and democracy in the classroom, would lead to better educational outcomes and prepare students for active citizenship in a democratic society. He also emphasized the importance of integrating practical skills and theoretical knowledge, contending that education should be a continuous process of growth and adaptation.

The relevance of Dewey's ideas in contemporary public education cannot be overstated. His emphasis on experiential learning, critical thinking, and democratic values has shaped the way we understand and approach education today.[4] Dewey's progressive educational philosophy highlights the importance of equipping students with the tools they need to become effective problem solvers and critical thinkers in an increasingly complex world. By nurturing these skills in a supportive and democratic learning environment, public education can better prepare students to be responsible, engaged citizens who can contribute meaningfully to society.[5] In this way, Dewey's contributions to the field of education continue to be highly relevant and valuable in the twenty-first century.

This is true for the PB project at VISD. Implementing PB in schools offers a valuable teaching opportunity for students, helping them learn about democratic processes and the importance of civic engagement. By involving students in established groups such as student councils, clubs, and honorary societies, schools can provide guidance and support for their participation in the budgeting process. More than one hundred years after Dewey first laid down these principles, they are still relevant to our ongoing efforts today in public education.

As Marguerite Roza wrote in her July 2021[6] *Forbes* article, "Will the American Rescue Plan's 'Meaningful Consultation' Requirement Usher in Community Participation in School Budgets?": "One question is whether [it is possible] . . . to change the process by which thousands of districts decide how to spend billions in school funds. Old habits die hard. And, let's be honest, there are a lot of vested interests when it comes to school spending." This question is a clarion call for a new way of thinking about budgeting. On a grander scale, this book is a call for a new way of thinking about transformation within our schools writ large.

LEADERSHIP: WHAT DOES IT DO?

Revisiting the inquiry at the onset of this chapter, one must consider whether the PB project was a good thing. Was the leadership exhibited by the superintendent, project manager, or board of education good or bad? Framing the question in this manner engenders a false dichotomy. Through extensive experience with leadership students, it has become evident that employing good and bad evaluative frameworks can be misleading and detract from the fundamental question warranting exploration.

Rather than appraising leadership on a binary scale, it is more constructive to examine its functional aspect. This approach entails assessing leadership in terms of its efficacy and impact, thus posing the question, "What does it do?" By reframing the discourse surrounding leadership, one can better elucidate the consequences of specific leadership styles and decisions, allowing for a more nuanced understanding of their role in shaping organizational outcomes. This shift in perspective facilitates a more comprehensive analysis, transcending the limitations imposed by the false dichotomy of good versus bad leadership.

There are countless ways to frame the VISD PB project to answer this question. Did VISD create an equitable funding structure to spend down remaining ESSER funds? Yes. Did VISD create a deeper sense of ownership around decision-making, specifically with students and staff? Yes. There are myriad ways to frame this leadership question to give evidence of leadership, which we may call good. In the framework section of this chapter however, three perceived failures of leadership were shared. What did leadership do in these instances? Cause confusion, drive some students away from the process, limit overall impact, and so on. We may feel inclined to label these outcomes as bad. The answer to the question, was this good or bad leadership, is that the question is irrelevant. By asking what did it do, we are able to have a more robust and nuanced conversation around impact and outcomes.

To have these conversations about leadership, it is incumbent on us to create and maintain a culture where innovation can thrive. The PB project was an innovative approach, among many others taking place at VISD. Unfortunately, although it is often a stated goal of a school district, very rarely does true innovation happen at a systemic level. We must ask why and what is the role of the leader.

As previously stated, a judgment culture in education is pervasive. We find it in policies, practices, and daily interactions. Judgment comes to us in the form of accountability. There are many facets to this accountability and judgment paradigm, and it often rears its head in ways we may not overtly recognize. Judgment creates a compliance culture. A compliance culture is exactly the opposite culture needed for innovation. You may be wondering why does a compliance culture work against innovation. The answer is relatively simple. Failure = blame. When failure is coupled with blame, people become hesitant to change and try new things. People will actively avoid innovation. People will stop asking "what if" and start asking "how." In public education, we have been working hard for nearly forty years to institute an accountability, judgment, and compliance culture into nearly everything we do from hiring, to renovating, to budgeting, to teaching, and testing, and learning. It stifles creativity and forestalls anything resembling true innovation. Only by decoupling failure from blame can we start to build a culture where failing (and by extension, learning) is celebrated.

Creating a culture where failure is celebrated in public education is not nearly as difficult as you might imagine. It starts with the superintendent and their association with data. Data (for anything) is always to be used as a flashlight and never to be used as a hammer. The first time you use data as a hammer, you have ensured you will never get accurate data ever again. People will begin to focus on self-preservation over sharing of information. This is especially true when the data are bad. In those moments, great leaders celebrate. They autopsy good data and bad data the same way, by asking what can be learned from the outcome. This will manifest itself at the board table and will be discussed further in the next chapter.

NOTES

1. Shepherd, "Participatory Budgeting."
2. Dewey, *Democracy and Education*.
3. Dewey, *Experience and Education*.
4. Noddings, *Philosophy of Education*.
5. Dewey, *Democracy and Education*, note 2.
6. Roza, "Will the American Rescue Plan's 'Meaningful Consultation' Requirement Usher in Community Participation in School Budgets?"

Chapter 9

Final Thoughts for Board Members

In the previous chapter, you read parting thoughts and considerations for superintendents. While some of those thoughts are applicable to board members, others are not. Closing this book with a chapter dedicated to board members seems most appropriate because the five-step framework described throughout this book is, in large part, the work of the board. It requires governance at the highest level.

Without a doubt, if you are a board member and reading this book, your district is likely engaged in some transformational or innovative effort. The outcome of that effort largely depends on the foundation on which they are building the programs. Without a solid foundation, they are nearly all destined for failure. As trustees, it is not your job to work on the top half of the graphic used throughout this book. If that book is ever written, it will be written for teacher leaders, principals, and superintendents. That book will be for the people doing the day-to-day work leading schools. That work is a management function and requires leadership and vision.

Your work as board members (and with the superintendent) is the bottom half of the graphic, which has been the focus of this book. You cannot do it alone. You must do this work as a unified "Team of 8." Doing this work with fidelity creates an unbreakable bedrock foundation on which nearly any transformational effort can be developed and achieved. This requires a governance mindset and a leadership focus.

In this chapter, we will examine the role of the board member in the theory of action process, paying special attention to the role of the board member as it relates to either the scope of the project or size of the district. We will also reframe participatory budgeting (PB) as a thinking framework a provide some thoughts about how a board member might use this framework to be a thinking partner with your superintendent in the transformational structures being built within the district. Next will be a brief exploration into seeing the bigger picture and how to apply this framework to your daily thinking. Finally, we will revisit goals and purposes and end with a brief discussion of governance and a call to action.

LEADERSHIP: WHAT DOES IT DO?

The previous chapter closed with leadership as a question of function by asking what does it do? This chapter opens with the same question. What does your leadership do? What impact are you making in the lives of students and teachers? As you serve our community in the vital role of leading our educational institutions, you face numerous complex and challenging decisions daily. These decisions have far-reaching impacts on the lives of our students, teachers, and the wider community. As you navigate this responsibility, you are urged to embrace the importance of mental frameworks for effective decision-making. The key takeaway from this book is one small sliver in helping you advance your personal leadership and the leadership of your school district by offering one mental model for building the supportive systemic structures that allow from transformational change to occur within our schools. To put this framework into practice, this is what it will require as you create a more robust, adaptable, and successful school system:

- Systems Thinking: Recognize that the school district functions as a complex, interconnected system. Adopt a holistic perspective, considering how your decisions impact various stakeholders and how each decision fits into the larger educational ecosystem.
- Growth Mindset: Embrace a growth mindset, both individually and as a board. Encourage continuous learning, curiosity, and adaptability in the face of challenges. Recognize that setbacks and mistakes are opportunities for learning and growth.
- Empathy and Compassion: Foster a culture of empathy and compassion in your decision-making, considering the perspectives and emotions of students, teachers, parents, and community members. Understand the experiences of others to create a more inclusive and nurturing educational environment.
- Evidence-Based Decision-Making: Ground your decisions in reliable, relevant data and research. Seek out multiple sources of information and be open to adjusting your viewpoints and actions based on new evidence.
- Ethical Framework: Uphold a strong ethical framework, considering the moral implications of your decisions. Strive to act with integrity, fairness, and transparency, prioritizing the best interests of the entire school community.

- Collaboration and Inclusivity: Encourage open dialogue and collaboration among board members, staff, and community stakeholders. Foster a sense of inclusivity, ensuring that diverse perspectives are considered and valued in the decision-making process.
- Long-Term Vision: Develop a clear, long-term vision for the school district, and align your decisions with that vision. Consider the future consequences of your choices, prioritizing sustainable and impactful solutions.
- Agility and Adaptability: Remain agile and adaptable in your decision-making, recognizing that the educational landscape is ever-changing. Be open to revisiting past decisions and adapting to new circumstances to ensure the ongoing success of the school district.
- Critical Thinking and Reflection: Engage in critical thinking and reflection, questioning assumptions, and challenging the status quo. Encourage robust discussions and debates to arrive at the best possible decisions.
- Balance and Prioritization: Balance competing interests and priorities while making decisions. Recognize that resources are limited and strive to allocate them in a manner that best serves the needs of the entire school community.

By embracing and using these concepts, you will be better equipped to make effective decisions that positively impact our students, staff, and community. Your commitment to these principles will create a thriving educational environment, preparing our children for a bright and successful future. We need you now more than ever.

BOARD GOVERNANCE AND TRANSFORMATIONAL LEADERSHIP IN PUBLIC EDUCATION

Public education plays a crucial role in shaping the future of any society, with schools serving as institutions that mold the minds of generations to come. The governance of these educational institutions is thus of paramount importance, impacting not only the education sector but also the wider social, economic, and political landscape. Board governance in public education refers to the systems, processes, and relationships that define the roles, responsibilities, and decision-making of a school board. We will now explore the nature of board governance roles in public education, providing examples of governance thinking. We will also examine the connection between board governance and leadership. As with the previous chapter, we will address the question, "what does leadership do?" and discuss its functional aspect in the context of a governance mindset.

Board governance in public education is a complex and multidimensional concept, encompassing a range of roles and responsibilities. Some key functions of school boards include setting strategic direction, establishing policies, monitoring the performance of the educational institution, and ensuring accountability.[1] Examples of governance thinking in public education can be found in the formulation of policies related to student achievement, teacher evaluation, and resource allocation. Effective board governance is characterized by a focus on student outcomes, data-driven decision-making, and collaborative relationships with stakeholders.[2]

To understand the connection between board governance and leadership, we must first have a leadership definition in mind. For the purposes of this book, we use Shepherd's definition of leadership[3] that posits that leadership is "the art and science of influencing others to willingly work together to achieve a common purpose or goal." In the context of board governance, this definition emphasizes the importance of collaboration, shared vision, and collective action. Transformational leadership, as outlined by Shepherd, involves four key components: idealized influence, inspirational motivation, intellectual stimulation, and individualized consideration. These elements can be applied to the board governance context by emphasizing the need for ethical conduct, setting high expectations, promoting innovation, and addressing the diverse needs of stakeholders.

Never forget that an influence relationship first requires a relationship. If you have no influence in a group, you cannot get that group to do much of anything. You cannot change a group if you are not part of that group. Once you become part of that group, you must earn your influence. The quickest way to earn that influence is by staying humble. The team will not care if you have the right answers, but they will absolutely care if you are asking the right questions.

As described in the previous chapter, leadership, in essence, is a question of function. It involves identifying and addressing the needs of the organization and its members, guiding the institution toward the achievement of shared goals, and fostering an environment of collaboration and innovation. In the context of board governance in public education, leadership functions include setting strategic direction, establishing policies, monitoring the performance of the educational institution, and ensuring accountability.[4] By adopting a governance mindset, leaders in public education can effectively navigate the challenges of the twenty-first century, ensuring that schools continue to serve as engines of social, economic, and political progress.

Board governance in public education is an essential component of effective leadership, with the roles and responsibilities of school boards encompassing a wide range of functions. By embracing the principles of transformational leadership and adopting a governance mindset, leaders in public education can create an environment that fosters collaboration, innovation, and excellence, which benefits students, educators, and the wider community. Understanding and implementing effective board governance in public education is crucial to the overall success of educational institutions. This, in turn, will ensure that schools continue to serve as agents of positive change within their communities, ultimately shaping a brighter future for all.

WHERE DID THE PROJECT REALLY START?

In the previous chapter, you read the PB project started with a question about spending down the remaining ESSER funds. This wasn't entirely true. The genesis for this project began many years ago when the Victoria Independent School District (VISD) trustees set out on a path of continuous improvement and building a culture where transformation can thrive. Although there were many small moves to start the process of building this culture, a pivotal moment came in 2019 when the board adopted a resolution stating, in part, they would treat complex and complicated problems differently. Complicated problems always have one right answer, and there is just one way to do the job. Lots of the work we do in education is complicated. This is not the work of the board. This is the work of the staff. Complex problems are inherently unknowable. There is never one right way and never one right answer. The level of disagreement in the room is usually a good barometer for the level of complexity in a problem. VISD became disciplined by passing this resolution that complex decisions will be taken directly to the people who will be most impacted first before any solution is even considered. Problems and not answers would be presented to the community. By committing through resolution, the board led with humility and vulnerability. Further, they made it possible for the superintendent and leadership team to do the same.

As board members this is a terrifying way to lead. It means admitting you do not have all the answers to all the questions being asked. It means that as task forces work through problems, they may have more information than you. It means that you may not have a solid grasp of what is happening on the dance floor because you are focused on the balcony view. This begs a question that must be answered before you can finish the remainder of this chapter.

Is yours a "managing board" or a "governing board?" It is a straightforward question. All public education boards may espouse, and even believe, they are governing boards. In truth, some (perhaps many) are functioning as a managing board. A managing board will often find itself during board meetings "in the weeds," asking detailed questions of administrators or presenters. They will often find themselves talking about parking lots, building renovations, teacher schedules, hiring challenges, fields, ball diamonds, purchasing buses, and so on. These are easy topics to talk about, and one can make an argument they are all complicated. They are certainly all management functions and only loosely connected to leadership, much less, governance.

A governing board, on the other hand, holds themselves to a different standard. A governing board asks, what is the role of mental health in the academic achievement within our low-socioeconomic-status student body in elementary school (focus on outcomes)? How are we as a district learning more (data as a flashlight, never as a hammer)? Does our budget support the discovery of this answer and an eventual plan to remedy (equitable funding)? How will we know if it is working (quality assurance)? Who will be involved in helping inform our decision (ownership)? What does this mean for policy if anything (courageous leadership)? Make special note, the board is asking questions and not giving answers. Make note, the board is not demanding excuses from administration but is seeking an explanation. A transformational governing board knows how to lead transformation with compassion.

To be sure, nearly every board has some members who are acting in a governance board mindset, and members who may be acting in a managing board mindset. At the end of the meeting, however, your board is speaking with one voice. That one voice is the majority of your members. In the following sections, the theory of action and the framework will be briefly explored from a governance perspective.

THEORY OF ACTION: IF-THEN

If board members are in regular contact with their superintendent, then it allows for an open flow of ideas. The ideation of remaining ESSER dollars came as a result of a simple phone call. Once the administration has estimated the remaining ESSER funding available (e.g., 5 percent), then they have a funding target to work with. By supporting the superintendent in implementing the theory of action described in this book, school board members help contribute to an equitable distribution of these funds, ensuring that access to resources and supports is widespread and transparent. Once the rough idea of a plan was coming together, this was shared with the full board for transparency and feedback.

In the example from the previous chapter, if a plan emerged to purchase an online tutoring program and once that plan is shared, it is incumbent on the board to ask if this is an equitable use of funding. Great governance board members can help identify potential gaps in access, such as internet availability and parental support in using technology. They can also contribute to discussions on alternative solutions to address these issues, thereby adding value to the conversation. Note that board members aren't doing the work and are not coming up with solutions; they are asking "wonder" questions. Remember, equity of opportunity is a path toward equality of outcome. Equity means advocating for the students who do not have people in their lives who can advocate on their behalf.

Furthermore, a school board member can be involved in ensuring that decisions made about the use of funds are rooted in equity and access by participating in discussions about quality assurance. They can help address questions about the desired outcomes, timelines, project effectiveness, and impact, as well as ensure that there is a clear framework for PB in place. Quality assurance does not mean using data as a hammer. Quality assurance is thinking about data as a flashlight. There is a quick way you can know as a board member what type of data culture you have in your district and is easy to remember using kindergarten parlance. At your board meetings, is it a culture of hide-and-seek or show-and-tell? This simple question (and answer) tells you everything you need to know about your data culture and ability to lead with quality assurance.

In supporting the superintendent, board members can also advocate for ownership of the decision-making process among various stakeholders, including principals, teachers, and students. By promoting the involvement of all relevant parties, they can foster a sense of shared responsibility and commitment to the success of the project. Ownership is simple to detect. Simply listen for its opposite, which are words like "*buy-in*" or "*engagement.*" As described previously in this book, these terms are the near enemy of true ownership. When you hear them, you have work to do.

School board members can further contribute by showcasing courageous leadership and policymaking. By accompanying students and staff to present the PB project at conferences and forums, they demonstrate their commitment to innovative and democratic decision-making processes in education. Simply ask yourself, when was the last time our board made a courageous decision?

Finally, a school board member can play a significant role in cultivating public will and understanding for transformation by sharing their experiences and knowledge with others. By encouraging conversations about PB and the theory of action, they help create an environment conducive to lasting change.

A school board member's involvement and support can be instrumental in implementing a successful PB project. By focusing on equity, quality assurance, stakeholder involvement, and courageous leadership, they add value to the conversation and help ensure the best possible outcomes for their school district.

The board member's role is active on two fronts. First, support the work and maintain an understanding of the theory of action. Second, engage as an active thought partner with the superintendent. As you read in the previous chapter, the superintendent is ever refocusing and running stairs. Sometimes, just one well-worded and thoughtful question can be a golden nugget for a superintendent in the ability to step back and detach from the daily work. It almost never comes in the form of a directive or a "want from you" conversation. It nearly always comes in the form of a question/wondering and in a "want for you" conversation. The paradigm shift is profound and makes all the difference for any chance of success.

THINKING FRAMEWORK

Using this cognitive framework, as delineated in the preceding chapter, necessitates the active engagement of board members in promoting an environment where administration and staff can conduct nonjudgmental critical analyses of past actions. Similar to the challenges faced by superintendents, mastering this approach demands considerable practice and perseverance. A crucial aspect of this process involves the objective evaluation of projects, devoid of judgmental biases. Introducing judgment into the analysis often leads to a proliferation of excuses, which inhibit the cultivation of a growth-oriented culture. Contrarily, providing explanations facilitates progress toward the intended goals.

Employing this cognitive tool effectively can help surmount obstacles that hinder project development. To illustrate this, consider a project that has either stagnated or has not been discussed for an extended period. Reflect on the circumstances surrounding the project and the individuals responsible for its current state. Upon recounting this narrative to oneself, attempt to retell the story from the perspective of bearing sole responsibility for the outcomes. In most instances, the initial account will be laden with judgment, whereas the latter rendition will be devoid of it. However, articulating the second narrative is considerably more challenging.

In the previous chapter, various areas warranting improvement were identified and examined. At this juncture, a board member's role in governance entails serving as an intellectual collaborator with the superintendent. Should the superintendent be unfamiliar with this text, it is advisable to provide them with a copy and initiate a meaningful discourse. It is essential for board members to adopt a supportive and constructive approach rather than resorting to judgment or disparagement.

By incorporating this cognitive tool into their interactions with the superintendent, board members can transition from a "closed and knowing" mindset to one that is "open and learning." It is a natural human tendency to approach conversations with preconceived notions and a sense of certainty. Exceptional board members acknowledge this propensity and strive to adopt an open-minded, inquisitive approach, which fosters curiosity, creativity, and encouragement. Consequently, this mindset paves the way for more effective collaboration with the superintendent, ultimately promoting a culture of growth and learning.

SEE THE BIGGER PICTURE: COMPREHENSIVE PERSPECTIVE

The notion of seeing the bigger picture is of paramount importance for school board members as well as superintendents. This perspective was evident at the culmination of the PB project at VISD, where the superintendent, principal project lead, board president, and a trustee convened to discuss the project's implications for the school board and future policy decisions. Their conversation touched on various aspects, including considerations of equity and budget planning. The previous chapter introduced the concept of step back and reframe, and the aforementioned meeting exemplified such a conversation, marking a pivotal moment in leadership and governance.

In the previous chapter, the superintendent's role is metaphorically likened to running stairs between the dance floor (i.e., the realm of management and day-to-day operations) and the balcony (i.e., the realm of strategic thinking and policymaking). This duality is essential, as it challenges the superintendent to reconcile the perspectives from the dance floor with those of the board members situated on the balcony. However, this juxtaposition is only relevant if board members maintain their position on the balcony. A board that is wholly immersed in the dance floor, functioning as a managing board, risks losing sight of the broader perspective.

To illustrate this point, consider a scenario involving a local grocery store. Suppose that, on visiting the store, you discover that the produce aisle lacks broccoli, carrots, and celery. The situation worsens the following week when even fewer vegetables are available. In such cases, customers typically seek resolution by contacting the produce manager, store manager, or customer service department. It would be highly unusual to reach out to the grocery store's board of directors for answers to specific operational issues because they likely lack detailed knowledge of day-to-day store management.

However, if the produce shortage affects multiple stores within a specific region, the issue transcends a single store's operations and becomes a matter of concern for the board of directors. In this context, a crucial question for discerning board members is: When does a customer complaint evolve into an owner's concern? This query highlights the importance of maintaining a comprehensive perspective and resisting the temptation to delve into specific customer complaints.

Education boards often face similar challenges because they may not possess detailed knowledge of the daily operations within schools. Despite this, educational institutions are frequently held to different standards than other organizations, such as grocery stores or hospitals. In many communities, school districts are the largest employers and function as major corporations. Yet, society often perceives education as distinct from other industries for two primary reasons.

First, people view school districts as smaller, more community-oriented entities compared to national grocery store chains. However, this argument loses credibility when one compares education boards to local or county hospital boards. Hospital board members are not expected to possess intricate knowledge of medical practices, nursing schedules, or cafeteria operations, despite their establishments often being smaller than school districts. Thus, size is not a valid justification for the disparate treatment of education boards.

Second, individuals often assume familiarity with education due to their personal experiences as students. However, this familiarity does not equate to expertise. Just as personal experience with automobiles or airplanes does not qualify one to manage an auto shop or airport, familiarity with education does not make one an expert in school operations or teaching methodologies. This fallacious thinking leads to unrealistic expectations for school board members, complicating board governance.

Ultimately, it is vital to foster a broader understanding that boards of education are similar to other industry boards, such as airport boards, hospital boards, or grocery store boards. By embracing this perspective, school board members can maintain a strategic focus, resist the allure of the dance floor, and fulfill their crucial roles in educational leadership and governance.

IN CLOSING: A LETTER, A CLARION CALL, A MANIFESTO TO EACH OF YOU

Dear Esteemed School Board Members,

As you embark on your journey as guardians and stewards of our community's education, it is vital to recognize the essential role you play in shaping the future of our children. Your leadership, dedication, and vision will make a difference in the lives of students, staff, parents, and the entire community. In that spirit, we present to you an inspirational message and manifesto to guide your actions and decisions as you lead our school district to new heights.

1. Embrace open dialogue and effective communication to bring the public back to public education. Strive to be great listeners and remain conscious of your verbal and nonverbal communication.
2. Act with deep compassion toward all stakeholders in the school community. Embrace the challenges and opportunities that arise and suffer together as we work toward our shared goals.
3. Understand that some situations are complicated, while others are complex, requiring a pragmatic approach and comfort with ambiguity. Trust the information you receive and be mindful that decisions may often be made in the gray areas.
4. Practice humility and approach every situation with a learning mindset. Recognize that you cannot be an expert in all matters, and this openness will garner the respect of your peers.
5. Devote yourself to relentless professional development and reading. Encourage your fellow board members to do the same, fostering a culture of growth and learning.
6. Stay informed about the ever-shifting political, legal, and economic landscape of public education. Work together to navigate these changes for the betterment of our community.
7. Be fair, consistent, decisive, and honest in all your dealings. Uphold these values as the cornerstones of your leadership.
8. Model exceptional governance and board presence. Seek regular feedback from your fellow board members to continuously improve your performance.
9. Prepare diligently for each board meeting and respect your superintendent's preparations by avoiding surprises.
10. Cultivate a thick skin, a titanium backbone, and an iron stomach. Your resilience and strength will guide the district through challenging times.
11. Strive for improvement, not perfection. Embrace the path of continuous growth and stay disciplined as you work together to achieve your goals.

In conclusion, remember that your actions and decisions impact the lives of many. Your commitment, passion, and dedication will shape the future of our children and our community. Stand united in your pursuit of excellence and remain steadfast in your mission to foster a brighter tomorrow for all.

With warmest regards and best wishes for your continued success,
The Community and Supporters of Public Education

NOTES

1. National School Boards Association, "Key Work of School Boards."
2. Rushton and Campbell, "Leading the Local School Board."
3. Shepherd, *The Secret to Transformational Leadership*.
4. National School Boards Association, "Key Work of School Boards."

Bibliography

Accrediting Commission for Schools, Western Association of Schools and Colleges. (2019). "Accreditation Criteria." https://www.acswasc.org/wp-content/uploads/2019/01/ACS-WASC-Accreditation-Criteria-2017.pdf
Ajzen, Icek. "The Theory of Planned Behavior." *Organizational Behavior and Human Decision Processes* 50, no. 2 (1991): 179–211.
Amabile, T. M. "Motivating Creativity in Organizations: On Doing What You Love and Loving What You Do." *California Management Review* 40, no. 1 (1997): 39–58.
American Institutes for Research. (2016). "Quality Assurance Review Process: Overview and Case Studies of Implementation in Four Districts." https://www.air.org/sites/default/files/downloads/report/Quality_Assurance_Review_Process.pdf
Austin Independent School District. (2017). "Austin ISD Equity Action Plan." https://www.austinisd.org/equity-action-plan
———. (2022). "Equity Policy." https://www.austinisd.org/equity
Avolio, B. J., and F. J. Yammarino. *Transformational and Charismatic Leadership: The Road Ahead*. Oxford: Oxford University Press, 2013.
Baiocchi, G. *Militants and Citizens: The Politics of Participatory Democracy in Porto Alegre*. Stanford, CA: Stanford University Press, 2005.
Baiocchi, G., and E. Ganuza. "Participatory Budgeting as if Emancipation Mattered." *Politics & Society* 42, no. 1 (2014): 29–50. https://doi.org/10.1177/0032329213512975
Baker, B. D., and S. P. Corcoran. (2012). "The Stealth Inequities of School Funding: How State and Local School Finance Systems Perpetuate Inequitable Student Spending." *Center for American Progress*. https://www.americanprogress.org/issues/education-k-12/reports/2012/09/19/38189/the-stealth-inequities-of-school-funding/
Baker, B. D., D. G. Sciarra, and D. Farrie. (2016). "Is School Funding Fair? A National Report Card." *Education Law Center*.
Baker, E. L., and R. L. Linn. "High-Stakes Testing Policies: Implications for Students, Teachers, and School Communities." *Educational Researcher* 42, no. 2 (2013): 69–78.

Baltimore City Public Schools. (n.d.) "Quality Assurance Review (QAR)." https://www.baltimorecityschools.org/Page/24284

Bass, B. M., and R. E. Riggio. *Transformational Leadership*, 2nd ed. London: Psychology Press, 2006.

Biesta, G. *Good Education in an Age of Measurement: Ethics, Politics, Democracy*. Boulder, CO: Paradigm Publishers, 2010.

Boser, U., and P. Baffour. (2021). "Isolated and Segregated: A New Look at the Income Divide in Our Nation's Schooling System." *Center for American Progress*. https://www.americanprogress.org/issues/education-k-12/reports/2021/02/25/496114/isolated-segregated/

Bronfenbrenner, Urie. *The Ecology of Human Development*. Cambridge, MA: Harvard University Press, 1979.

Brown, B. *Dare to Lead: Brave Work. Tough Conversations. Whole Hearts.* New York: Random House, 2018.

Bryk, A. S., and B. Schneider. "Trust in Schools: A Core Resource for School Reform." *Educational Leadership* 60, no. 6 (2002): 40–45.

———. *Trust in Schools: A Core Resource for Improvement*. New York: Russell Sage Foundation, 2003.

Bryk, A. S., P. B. Sebring, E. Allensworth, S. Luppescu, and J. Q. Easton. *Organizing Schools for Improvement: Lessons from Chicago*. Chicago: University of Chicago Press, 2010.

Bush, T., and L. Bell. *The Principles and Practice of Educational Management*. London: Paul Chapman, 2002.

Cabannes, Y. "Participatory Budgeting: A Significant Contribution to Participatory Democracy." *Environment and Urbanization* 16, no. 1 (2004), 27–46. doi.org/10.1177/095624780401600104

———. "The Impact of Participatory Budgeting on Basic Services: Municipal Practices and Evidence from the Field." *Environment and Urbanization* 27, no. 1 (2015): 257–84.

California Department of Education. (2021). "California School Dashboard." https://www.caschooldashboard.org/

Center for Public Education. (2009). "School Boards Matter: The Evidence behind the Headlines." https://www.centerforpubliceducation.org/system/files/2010/01/School_Boards_Matter.pdf

Cheng, Y. C., and W. M. Tam. Multi-Models of Quality in Education. *Quality Assurance in Education*, 5, no. 1 (1997): 22–31.

Chubb, J. E. "Why Public Will Is Crucial in Education Reform." *Education Next* 15, no. 2 (2015): 16–22.

City of Boston. (2014). "Youth Lead the Change: Participatory Budgeting Boston." https://www.boston.gov/departments/youth-engagement-and-employment/youth-lead-change-participatory-budgeting Boston.

City of Seattle. (2017). "Youth Voice, Youth Choice: Participatory Budgeting Results." https://www.seattle.gov/neighborhoods/programs-and-services/youth-voice-youth-choice

City of Vallejo. (2013). "Participatory Budgeting Vallejo: The First Citywide PB Process in the United States." https://www.ci.vallejo.ca.us/common/pages/DisplayFile.aspx?itemId=29513

Collins, J. *Good to Great: Why Some Companies Make the Leap . . . and Others Don't.* New York: Harper Business, 2001.

Council for Higher Education Accreditation. (2018). "CHEA Recognition Policy and Procedures." https://www.chea.org/sites/default/files/CHEA_Recognition_Policy_and_Procedures_2018.pdf

Covey, S. R. *The 7 Habits of Highly Effective People: Powerful Lessons in Personal Change.* New York: Free Press, 2004.

Dahl, R. A. *On Democracy.* Princeton, NJ: Yale University Press, 1998.

Darling-Hammond, L. *The Flat World and Education: How America's Commitment to Equity Will Determine Our Future.* New York: Teachers College Press, 2010.

———. "The Problems with Testing and Accountability." *Phi Delta Kappan* 96, no. 6 (2015): 8–14.

Darling-Hammond, L., G. Wilhoit, and L. Pittenger. "Accountability for College and Career Readiness: Developing a New Paradigm." *Education Policy Analysis Archives* 22 (2014): 1–32. https://doi.org/10.14507/epaa.v22.1673

Deci, E. L., and R. M. Ryan. "The 'What' and 'Why' of Goal Pursuits: Human Needs and the Self-Determination of Behavior." *Psychological Inquiry* 11, no. 4 (2000): 227–68.

Deming, W. E. *Out of the Crisis.* Cambridge, MA: Massachusetts Institute of Technology Center for Advanced Engineering Study, 1986.

Dewey, J. *Democracy and Education.* New York: Simon & Brown, 1916/2011.

———. *Experience and Education.* New York: Touchstone, 1938/1997.

Dintersmith, T. *What Schools Could Be: Insights and Inspiration from Teachers across America.* Princeton, NJ: Princeton University Press, 2018.

Dougherty, C., and N. F. Hurd. *Closing the Opportunity Gap: What America Must Do to Give Every Child an Even Chance.* New York: Teachers College Press, 2016.

Duncan-Andrade, J. (2015). "What Is Equity in Education?" *Edutopia.* https://www.edutopia.org/blog/what-is-equity-in-education-joseph-duncan

Education Commission of the States. (2016). "Can School Funding Reform Help Close the Achievement Gap?" https://www.ecs.org/can-school-funding-reform-help-close-the-achievement-gap/

———. (2019). "School Finance Litigation: An Overview." https://www.ecs.org/school-finance-litigation-an-overview/

Education Week. (2023). "Poorer Districts Were More Likely to Use COVID Relief Money to Repair Buildings." https://www.edweek.org/leadership/poorer-districts-were-more-likely-to-use-covid-relief-money-to-repair-buildings/2023/02

Epstein, J. L., M. G. Sanders, B. S. Simon, K. C. Salinas, N. R. Jansorn, and F. L. Van Voorhis. *School, Family, and Community Partnerships: Your Handbook for Action.* Thousand Oaks, CA: Corwin Press, 2002.

Evans, A. "Public Will and Education Reform: How Public Opinion Shapes Education Policy." *Education Policy Analysis Archives* 26, no. 53 (2018). https://doi.org/10.14507/epaa.26.3481

Fullan, M. *Leading in a Culture of Change*. San Francisco, CA: Jossey-Bass, 2001.
———. *The New Meaning of Educational Change*, 4th ed. New York: Teachers College Press, 2007.
———. *Leading in a Culture of Change*. New York: John Wiley & Sons, 2014.
———. *The Principal: Three Keys to Maximizing Impact*. New York: John Wiley & Sons, 2014.
Fung, A. "Varieties of Participation in Complex Governance." *Public Administration Review* 66, no. 1 (2006): 66–75.
Fung, A., and E. O. Wright. "Thinking about Empowered Participatory Governance." In A. Fung and E. O. Wright (eds.), *Deepening Democracy: Institutional Innovations in Empowered Participatory Governance* (pp. 3–42). New York: Verso, 2023.
García, E., and E. Weiss. (2019). "School Funding and Student Success: A Review of the Literature." *Economic Policy Institute*. https://www.epi.org/publication/school-funding-and-student-success-a-review-of-the-literature/
Gay, G. *Culturally Responsive Teaching: Theory, Research, and Practice*. New York: Teachers College Press, 2000.
George, M. L., D. Rowlands, M. Price, and J. Maxey. *The Lean Six Sigma Pocket Toolbook: A Quick Reference Guide to 100 Tools for Improving Quality and Speed*. New York: McGraw-Hill, 2005.
Gilman, H. R. "Engaging Citizens: Participatory Budgeting and the Inclusive Governance Movement within the United States." *Public Administration Review* 76, no. 1 (2016): 50–59.
Goetsch, D. L., and S. B. Davis. *Quality Management for Organizational Excellence*. Upper Saddle River, NJ: Pearson, 2014.
Goldfrank, B. *Deepening Local Democracy in Latin America: Participation, Decentralization, and the Left*. University Park: Pennsylvania State University Press, 2012.
Goleman, D. "Leadership That Gets Results." *Harvard Business Review* 78, no. 2 (2000): 78–90.
Gonçalves, S. "The Effects of Participatory Budgeting on Municipal Expenditures and Infant Mortality in Brazil." *World Development* 53 (2014): 94–110.
González, N. "Community-Based Accountability and School Reform: A Comprehensive Review of the Literature." *Review of Educational Research* 86, no. 2 (2016): 561–99.
Guilford County Schools. (2018). "Strategic Plan." https://www.gcsnc.com/cms/lib/NC01910393/Centricity/Domain/4/GCS%20Strategic%20Plan%202018-2022.pdf
Gupta, A. Quality Assurance in Higher Education. *Journal of Education and Practice* 9, no. 28 (2018): 10–16.
Hargreaves, A., and M. Fullan. *Professional Capital: Transforming Teaching in Every School*. New York: Teachers College Press, 2012.
Harvey, L., and J. Newton. "Transforming Quality Evaluation: Moving On." In L. Harvey and J. Newton (eds.), *Transforming Quality Evaluation: Moving On* (pp. 1–30). Birmingham, UK: QHE Publications, 2004.
Headden, S. "Why School Transparency Is Important." *Education Next* 16, no. 1 (2016): 1–9.

Heifetz, R. A., and M. Linsky. *Leadership on the Line: Staying Alive through the Dangers of Leading.* Brighton, MA: Harvard Business Review Press, 2002.

Heifetz, R. A., A. Grashow, and M. Linsky. *The Practice of Adaptive Leadership: Tools and Tactics for Changing Your Organization and the World.* Brighton, MA: Harvard Business Press, 2009.

Henderson, A. T., and K. L. Mapp. (2002). "A New Wave of Evidence: The Impact of School, Family, and Community Connections on Student Achievement." *National Center for Family & Community Connections with Schools.*

Hill, C. "Transformational Leadership in the Era of Change." *Journal of Business Strategy* 38, no. 1 (2017): 33–39.

Ingersoll, R. M., and M. Strong. "The Impact of Induction and Mentoring Programs for Beginning Teachers: A Critical Review of the Research." *Review of Educational Research* 81, no. 2 (2011): 201–33. https://doi.org/10.3102/0034654311403323

Jennings, J., and D. S. Rentner. "Ten Big Effects of the No Child Left Behind Act on Public Schools." *Phi Delta Kappan* 88, no. 2 (2006): 110–13.

Jennings, P. A., and M. T. Greenberg. "The Prosocial Classroom: Teacher Social and Emotional Competence in Relation to Student and Classroom Outcomes." *Review of Educational Research* 79, no. 1 (2009): 491–525.

Juran, J. M. *A History of Managing for Quality.* Milwaukee, WI: ASQ Quality Press, 1995.

Juran, J. M., and A. B. Godfrey. *Juran's Quality Handbook*, 5th ed. New York: McGraw-Hill, 1998.

Kanter, R. M. "The Ten Commandments of Change Management." *Ivey Business Journal* 66, no. 1 (2012): 16–21.

Kettunen, J. "Implementation of Strategies in Continuing Education and Training: The Impact of Institutional and Social Context." *International Journal of Lifelong Education* 35, no. 1 (2016): 62–77.

Kober, N. "Public Opinion and Education Policy: The Role of Interest Groups, Ideology, and Information." *Educational Policy* 33, no. 1 (2019): 3–37. https://doi.org/10.1177/0895904817743721

Kotter, J. P. *Leading Change.* Brighton, MA: Harvard Business Review Press, 1996.

———. *Leading Change.* Brighton, MA: Harvard Business Press, 2012.

———. *The 8-Step Process for Leading Change.* Cambridge, MA: Kotter International, 2012.

Ku, H. Y., and A. Sullivan Palincsar. "Innovating Beyond the Traditional Classroom: The Potential of Partnerships for Learning." *The Journal of Educational Research* 114, no. 4 (2021): 343–53. doi: 10.1080/00220671.2020.1806032

Ladd, H. F., and D. L. Lauen. "Who Benefits from K–12 Education Subsidies? The Effects of Expanding Public Education in North Carolina." *The Annals of the American Academy of Political and Social Science* 629, no. 1 (2010): 198–214.

Lander, B. (2011). "Participatory Budgeting in District 39." https://council.nyc.gov/brad-lander/pb/2011/

Leithwood, K. "Transformational School Leadership for Large-Scale Reform: Effects on Students, Teachers, and Their Classroom Practices." *School Effectiveness and School Improvement* 27, no. 1 (2016): 57–79.

Leithwood, K., and K. S. Louis. *Linking Leadership to Student Learning.* New York: John Wiley & Sons, 2012.
Leithwood, K., and C. Riehl. *What We Know about Successful School Leadership.* Philadelphia: Laboratory for Student Success, Temple University, 2005.
Lerner, J., and D. Schugurensky. "Who Learns What from Participating in Participatory Budgeting? The Case of Rosario, Argentina." In *Learning Citizenship: Practical Teaching Strategies for Secondary Schools* (pp. 90–101). London: Continuum, 2007.
Lerner, J., and Secondo, D. "By the People, for the People: Participatory Budgeting from the Bottom up in North America." *Journal of Public Deliberation* 8, no. 2 (2012): Article 5.
Levkovitz, Y. (2021). "Participatory Budgeting in the United States: A Guide for Local Officials. National League of Cities." https://www.nlc.org/resource/participatory-budgeting-in-the-united-states-a-guide-for-local-officials/
Lubienski, C., and S. T. Lubienski. *The Public School Advantage: Why Public Schools Outperform Private Schools.* University of Chicago Press, 2014.
Madison Metropolitan School District. (2016). "High School Start Time Changes: Frequently Asked Questions." https://www.madison.k12.wi.us/sites/default/files/HS%20Start%20Times%20FAQ.pdf
Marzano, R. J., T. Waters, and B. A. McNulty. *School Leadership That Works: From Research to Results.* Alexandria, VA: ASCD, 2005.
McChesney, C., S. Covey, and J. Huling. *The 4 Disciplines of Execution: Achieving Your Wildly Important Goals.* New York: Free Press, 2012.
McDonnell, L. M., R. R. S. Socolar, and A. S. Kirschner. (2015). *A Path Forward: Improving Educator Preparation for Family Engagement and Student Learning.* Washington, DC: The Aspen Institute, 2015.
Middlehurst, R. "Quality Assurance Implications of New Forms of Higher Education." *European Journal of Education* 36, no. 3 (2001): 377–91.
Minneapolis Public Schools. (2022). "Equity Framework." https://equity.mpls.k12.mn.us/
Montgomery County Public Schools. (2019). "Math Program Review." https://www.montgomeryschoolsmd.org/departments/academics/curriculum/mathematics/math-review.aspx
———. (2022). "Equity Initiatives." https://www.montgomeryschoolsmd.org/departments/equity-initiatives/
Moore, J. "Participatory Budgeting: An Experiment in Democracy." *National Civic Review* 100, no. 3 (2011): 34–38.
Mullis, Ina V. S., et al. (2016). *TIMSS 2015 International Results in Mathematics.* Boston: Boston College, TIMSS & PIRLS International Study Center. http://timssandpirls.bc.edu/timss2015/international-results/
National Center for Education Evaluation and Regional Assistance. (2017). *Quality Assurance Review of Baltimore City Public Schools: Final Report.* https://ies.ed.gov/ncee/pubs/20174004/pdf/20174004.pdf
National Center for Education Statistics. (2022). *Revenues and Expenditures for Public Elementary and Secondary Education: FY 82–FY19 (NCES 2022-300).* Washington, DC: U.S. Department of Education.

National Commission on Excellence in Education. *A Nation at Risk: The Imperative for Educational Reform*. Washington, DC: U.S. Government Printing Office, 1983.

National Conference of State Legislatures. (2019). "School Funding 101." https://www.ncsl.org/research/education/school-funding-101.aspx

National Education Association. (2021). "Research on School Funding." https://www.nea.org/resource-library/research-school-funding

National Equity Project. (2022). "What Is Educational Equity?" https://nationalequityproject.org/what-is-equity/

National Public Radio. (2021). "The History of School Funding in the U.S." https://www.npr.org/2021/03/24/980871103/the-history-of-school-funding-in-the-u-s

National School Boards Association. (2010). "Key Work of School Boards: A Synthesis of Research on School Boards' Work in Improving Student Achievement." https://www.nsba.org/-/media/NSBA/File/research/keywork2010.pdf

———. (2019). "Building Community Support for Public Schools." https://www.nsba.org/advocacy/building-community-support-public-schools

———. (2019). "Governance and Leadership." https://www.nsba.org/About-School-Boards/Governance-and-Leadership

———. (2021). "Key Work of School Boards." https://www.nsba.org/Resources/Key-Work-of-School-Boards

National School Public Relations Association. (2019). "Communication and Community Engagement." https://www.nspra.org/communication-and-community-engagement

New York City Council. (2014). "Participatory Budgeting: Cycle 4 Report." https://council.nyc.gov/pb/wp-content/uploads/sites/55/2015/10/PB_Report_2015_FINAL_small.pdf

Nieto, S. *The Light in Their Eyes: Creating Multicultural Learning Communities*. New York: Teachers College Press, 2010.

Noddings, N. *Philosophy of Education*. Boulder, CO: Westview Press, 2015.

Oakland, J. S. *Total Quality Management and Operational Excellence: Text with Cases*. New York: Routledge, 2014.

OECD. (2013). "Synergies for Better Learning: An International Perspective on Evaluation and Assessment." *OECD Publishing*. https://doi.org/10.1787/9789264190658-en

Oregon Department of Education. (2019). "Oregon's Community-Based Accountability System." https://www.oregon.gov/ode/educator-resources/assessment/Pages/Oregons-Community-Based-Accountability-System.aspx

Owens, A. *Unequal City: Race, Schools, and Perceptions of Injustice*. New York: Russell Sage Foundation, 2016.

Palmer, P. J. *The Courage to Teach: Exploring the Inner Landscape of a Teacher's Life*. San Francisco, CA: Jossey-Bass, 1998.

Parmenter, D. *Key Performance Indicators: Developing, Implementing, and Using Winning KPIs*, 3rd ed. Hoboken, NJ: John Wiley & Sons, 2015.

Pateman, C. "Participatory Democracy Revisited." *Perspectives on Politics* 10, no. 1 (2012): 7–19. https://doi.org/10.1017/S1537592711004877

PB NYC. (2021). "Participatory Budgeting in New York City." https://pbnyc.org/

Phoenix Union High School District. (2015). "Participatory Budgeting." https://www.pxu.org/Page/18191
Pink, D. H. *Drive: The Surprising Truth about What Motivates Us*. New York: Riverhead Books, 2009.
Robinson, V. M. J., C. A. Lloyd, and J. K. Rowe. "The Impact of Leadership on Student Outcomes: An Analysis of the Differential Effects of Leadership Types." *Educational Administration Quarterly* 44, no. 5 (2008): 635–74.
Rost, J. C. *Leadership for the Twenty-First Century*. Westport, CT: Praeger Publishers, 1991.
Roza, M. (2017). "Funding Student-Centered Education Policy." *Center on Reinventing Public Education*. https://www.crpe.org/publications/funding-student-centered-education-policy
———. (2021). "Will the American Rescue Plan's 'Meaningful Consultation' Requirement Usher in Community Participation in School Budgets?" *Forbes Magazine*.
Rushton, G., and C. Campbell. "Leading the Local School Board: The Role and Function of Public School Board Chairs." *Journal of Research on Leadership Education* 13, no. 1 (2018): 10–26. doi: 10.1177/1942775117709535
Salovey, P., and J. D. Mayer. "Emotional Intelligence." *Imagination, Cognition and Personality*, 9, no. 3 (1990): 185–211. doi: 10.2190/DUGG-P24E-52WK-6CDG.
San Francisco Unified School District. "Culturally Responsive Teaching and Leading." https://www2.wested.org/www-static/online_pubs/rel/weighted-student-formula-summary.pdf
Seattle Public Schools. (2020). "COVID-19: Remote Learning." https://www.seattleschools.org/district/calendars/news/what_s_new/coronavirus_update/remote_learning
———. (2022). "Our Strategic Plan." https://www.seattleschools.org/about-us/strategic-plan/
Semega, Jessica, and Melissa Kollar. (2022). "Income in the United States: 2021." *Census.gov*. www.census.gov/library/publications/2022/demo/p60-276.html.
Shepherd, Quintin. *The Secret to Transformational Leadership*. New York: Compassionate Leadership LLC, 2021.
———. (2022). "Participatory Budgeting." *School Administrator*. https://my.aasa.org/AASA/Resources/SAMag/2022/Oct22/Shepherd.aspx
Shewhart, Walter A. *Economic Control of Quality of Manufactured Product*. New York: D. Van Nostrand Company, 1931.
Sinek, Simon. *Leaders Eat Last: Why Some Teams Pull Together and Others Don't*. New York: Portfolio/Penguin, 2014.
Sintomer, Y., C. Herzberg, and A. Röcke. "Participatory Budgeting in Europe: Potentials and Challenges." *International Journal of Urban and Regional Research* 32, no. 1 (2008): 164–78. https://doi.org/10.1111/j.1468-2427.2008.00777.x.
Smyth, J., B. Down, P. McInerney, and R. Hattam. "School Community Partnerships in Neoliberal Times." *Education as a Human Enterprise: Reclaiming the Sociological Imagination* 2014: 97–118. https://doi.org/10.1007/978-94-007-7974-0_6

Sousa, Maria João Machado, and Ricardo A. Ribeiro Ramos. (2019). "Quality Control in Education." In P. Isaias, T. Issa, and P. Kommers (eds.), *Proceedings of the 15th International Conference on Mobile Learning* (pp. 209–13).

Spillane, J. P., B. J. Reiser, and T. Reimer. "Policy Implementation and Cognition: Reframing and Refocusing Implementation Research." *Review of Educational Research* 72, no. 3 (2002): 387–431.

Su, Celina. "Does Participation in Participatory Budgeting Improve the Legitimacy of Local Government? A Comparative Study of New York City and Chicago." *Journal of Urban Affairs* 39, no. 6 (2017): 806–25.

Tanner, John. *Community-Based Accountability: A Paradigm for Measuring and Improving Education*. Lanham, MD: Rowman & Littlefield, 2014.

Texas Education Agency. (2018). "Community and Student Engagement." https://tea.texas.gov/student-assessment/accountability/community-and-student-engagement

Touchton, Michael, and Brian Wampler. "Improving Social Well-Being through New Democratic Institutions." *Comparative Political Studies* 47, no. 10 (2014).

US Census Bureau. (2023). "U.S. Census Bureau Quickfacts: Victoria City, Texas." www.census.gov/quickfacts/victoriacitytexas

Van Horn, Carrie. "A Comparison of Community-Based and Benefits-Based Accountability Systems." *Educational Policy* 32, no. 2 (2018): 231–56.

Wagner, R., and J. K. Harter. *12: The Elements of Great Managing*. New York: Gallup Press, 2006.

Wampler, B. *Participatory Budgeting in Brazil: Contestation, Cooperation, and Accountability*. University Park, PA: Pennsylvania State University Press, 2007.

Waters, T., and R. J. Marzano. *School District Leadership That Works: The Effect of Superintendent Leadership on Student Achievement*. Denver, CO: Mid-continent Research for Education and Learning, 2006.

Welner, K. G., and P. L. Carter, eds. *Closing the Opportunity Gap: What America Must Do to Give Every Child an Even Chance*. New York: Oxford University Press, 2013.

Willink, J., and L. Babin. *Extreme Ownership: How U.S. Navy SEALs Lead and Win*. New York: St. Martin's Press, 2015.

———. *The Dichotomy of Leadership: Balancing the Challenges of Extreme Ownership to Lead and Win*. New York: St. Martin's Press, 2018.

Acknowledgments

I would like to express my deepest gratitude to the numerous individuals who have played a significant role in the creation of this book. Writing a book on theories of action and frameworks for public school boards of education to bring about transformational change has been a labor of love, and I could not have done it without the support, insights, and expertise of many along the way.

First and foremost, I would like to extend my heartfelt appreciation to the dedicated members of the various boards of education with whom I have had the privilege of working alongside for nearly two decades. As a superintendent in four districts across three states, I have witnessed your unwavering commitment to the betterment of our schools and communities. Your collective wisdom, passion, and determination have been instrumental in shaping my understanding of the challenges and opportunities inherent in educational transformation.

I am most grateful for your willingness to let me try. So many superintendent colleagues are stifled by boards that are afraid of failure and unwilling to accept that real change is hard. I have been most fortunate to work with boards that embrace the unknown, commit to being a learning team, and were willing to just try. My two favorite words are, "I wonder . . . ." Your support made the wonder magic possible.

Each of you have been a big part of my learning journey: Lowell Beggs, Tom Mead, Joe Flessner, Dan Stephenitch, Bob Olson, Reed Akre, Tony Becker, Maggie Nessim, Lisa Kalhara, Mark Chao, Steve Dembo, Felicia Holtz, Barbera Poddig, Sajan Jose, Lisa Kaihara, Rebecca Abelson, George AbouAssaly, Cara Lausen, Clark Weaver, Rene Gadelha, Todd Hutcheson, Barry Buchholz, Estella De Los Santos, Mike DiSantos Margaret Pruett, Lou Svetlik, Kevin VanHook, Bret Baldwin, Mandy Lingle, and Kathy Bell. I purposely left a few names out. A superintendent forms an especially unique bond with their board president. Each of the presidents I have served with were willing to listen, think with me, challenge me, and inspire me in different ways. I want to give special recognition to Mark Becker, Lori Setchell, Zach Williams, Terri Lefler, Tim Isenberg, Mike Mercer, Ross Mansker, and Tami Keeling. I am forever in your debt.

I am also grateful for the insights and collaboration of my fellow superintendents, educators, and administrators, who have generously shared their experiences, ideas, and best practices with me. Your tireless work to create nurturing learning environments for all students is truly inspiring.

To the countless teachers, staff members, students, and families who make up our diverse school communities, thank you for entrusting me with the responsibility of leading and supporting your educational journeys. Your voices and stories have been invaluable in informing the ideas and strategies presented in this book.

I must also acknowledge the invaluable contributions of the editors and the publishing staff who have worked diligently to ensure the quality and clarity of this work. Special thanks to Ashley Scott for helping with the figures for this book. Your professionalism and attention to detail have been invaluable in bringing this book to fruition.

Lastly, I would like to express my love and gratitude to my wife, Sarah, for the endless support and willingness to listen to me ramble unremittingly about this topic I love so much. I would also like to express my love and gratitude to my children Vivian and Gwendolyn, who provided the daily inspiration to try to do great things for all kids. To my friends, thank you for your unwavering support and encouragement throughout this journey. Collectively, your belief in me and the importance of this work has been a source of strength and motivation.

In conclusion, I hope that this book will serve as a useful resource and guide for public school boards of education, superintendents, and all stakeholders invested in the transformative power of education. Together, we can build supportive systemic structures that enable districts, schools, and communities to thrive and reach their full potential.

About the Author

Dr. Quintin "Q" Shepherd is a distinguished leader in the field of education, amassing nearly two decades of service as a public-school superintendent across multiple states. Beginning his career journey in the humble role of school custodian, he has since held various crucial positions, including a PreK–12 music teacher, an elementary principal, and a high school principal.

Shepherd's exceptional leadership acumen and profound contributions to the educational sector are widely recognized. His multidimensional experience spanning from classroom teaching to administrative leadership provides him a unique perspective that has consistently fostered transformational change in the institutions he has served.

In addition to his esteemed role as a superintendent, Q also shares his wisdom and insights as an adjunct faculty member at the University of Houston-Victoria, guiding and inspiring the forthcoming generation of educational leaders. His expertise extends beyond the realms of academia, earning him a reputable status as an international speaker frequently sought after for his valuable insights on leading transformational change.

He is the respected author of the best-selling book *The Secret to Transformational Leadership*, which has garnered widespread acclaim for its in-depth exploration of effective leadership strategies. This work is universally acknowledged as a seminal reading for anyone aspiring to effect meaningful impact in the educational sphere.

Shepherd's commitment to nurturing leaders, his ongoing contribution to the educational discourse, and his impactful written work underscore his standing as a prominent figure in the field of education.

www.ingramcontent.com/pod-product-compliance
Lightning Source LLC
Chambersburg PA
CBHW020652300426
44112CB00007B/346